The Writer's
PRIMER

A Practical Guide
for Aspiring Authors
Seeking Publication

The Writer's
PRIMER

A Practical Guide
for Aspiring Authors
Seeking Publication

Roland Allnach

Published by Tabalt Press
PO Box 354
Kings Park, NY, 11754

ISBN 978-0-9967854-2-6

Editorial and layout services provided by Nancy Barnes, whose indispensable
skills and support helped bring this book to light.
www.storiestotellbooks.com

Contents

Part 4 Regarding Novels

Part 5 Regarding Marketing

Fiction by Roland Allnach

Prism

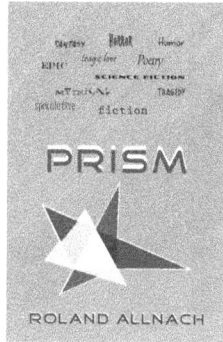

Prism collects seventeen stories into one volume and follows a trail of diverse genres and narrative forms. From literary fiction to speculative fiction, from humor to horror, from tragedy to mythical poetry, **Prism** presents a wide-ranging journey of contemplations on the human condition.

Silver Medal - Short Stories, 2015 Feathered Quill Book Awards

Winner - Short Stories, 2015 Pacific Book Review Book Awards

"Allnach delivers a wonderful collection of stories in Prism*."* **Lisa Jones, Readers' Favorite**

"A timeless, exquisite collection of short stories that's bound to leave you mesmerized and awestruck. The collection is a masterpiece." **Rattan Whig, Readers' Favorite**

"Allnach has a voice that speaks so loud readers lose themselves in the stories ... A dazzling collection." **Amy Lignor, Feathered Quill Reviews**

*"*Prism *is a book of stories written with precision ... it chisels out what is needed with laser description, true to the ear dialogue, characters built into believability, and stories that capture the attention. This collection is to be savored, read again and again."* **F.T. Donereau, Rebecca's Reads**

Oddities & Entities

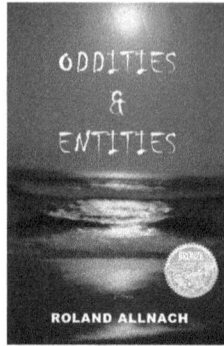

Oddities & Entities is a surreal, provocative anthology of six tales within the supernatural, paranormal, and horror genres, exploring a definition of life beyond the fragile vessel of the human body.

Oddities & Entities has been recognized with seven national book awards, with multiple awards from Readers' Favorite Book of the Year Awards and USA Book News Best Book Awards. Single awards include National Indie Excellence Awards, Foreword Reviews Book of the Year Awards, and Pacific Book Reviews Book Awards.

"If you only read one book this year, make it this one. Be prepared to have your comfort zone challenged." **Lee Ashford, Readers' Favorite**

"Allnach is a master storyteller with a powerful pen. The stories are gritty, gruesome, bewitching, and beautiful." **Cynthia Brian, NY Times Bestselling author and host of "Starstyle"**

"This is a great book. Nothing you expect to happen happens. The author keeps you thinking and turning the page over and over." **Jason Lulos, Pacific Book Review**

Remnant

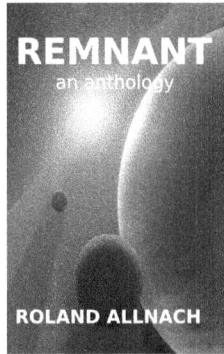

Remnant is a stirring, thought-provoking anthology of three novellas within the speculative and science fiction genres. Following a path from the shores of a doomed paradise, through an illusory reality, and ending in a devastated future, *Remnant* is both the sum of these tales and the element that binds them together.

Remnant has been recognized with four national book awards from National Indie Excellence Awards, Readers' Favorite Book of the Year Awards, USA Book News Best Book Awards, and Feathered Quill Book of the Year Awards.

"Each of the three novellas is a beautifully crafted gem of a story." **Douglas R. Cobb, Bestsellersworld.com**

"Allnach's writing style can be described as smart, elegant, and addicting." **San Francisco Book Review**

"Roland Allnach is destined to become recognized for his contributions in whatever genre of writing he may choose." **Richard R. Blake, Reader Views**

"With Remnant, *Roland Allnach presents three novellas that promise to haunt the readers long after the cover has been closed. A nearly perfect gem of sci-fi."* **Peter Dabbene, Foreword,** *Clarion Review*

Introduction

"You know, I have a great idea for a story ..."

FOR MANY AUTHORS, THIS SINGLE thought is the start of a complex journey. Today's publication world offers more opportunities than perhaps any previous time, thanks in large part to the Internet and the open accessibility of numerous self-publishing outlets. Online journals exist alongside print journals, small publishers and self-published authors are listed beside large publishers and A-list authors, and a wide array of bloggers and reading communities are looking for the next great author to follow. Nevertheless, with so many options and variables, the marketplace itself can be daunting.

The intention of this book is to introduce aspiring writers to the rich landscape of the publishing world. Whether you're looking to publish a story or book, or have yet to put a single word to paper—or keyboard—I've assembled this primer as a practical guide to the realities that await you. From basic considerations of how writing can find a place in your life to rudimentary mechanics of proper literary technique; from short story publication, book publication, and finally to marketing, this primer aims to provide you with a walking guide. Consider it a source of things you might wish to have known in hindsight, which is the perspective I took when deciding on the sections for each part of this book. The information shared in these pages would have been a very welcome companion when I took my first steps—or stumbles—into the publishing world.

In regard to semantics, I use the words 'primer' and 'guide' in the title and subtitle of this book for specific reasons. As a *primer* it's meant to introduce those unfamiliar with the publishing world to the situations they will most likely encounter; as a *guide* it's meant to give fundamental and practical advice on taking the first steps into that world. There are numerous books on writing and publishing, many of which claim to be definitive guides. Unfortunately, given the dynamic nature of the publishing world, any "definitive" publishing guide is most likely obsolete within a year of its own publication.

This primer is different from other how-to books in that I present material from the perspective of a fellow author in the trenches of the publishing industry. While there are many volumes offering advice from the upper reaches of success, few books address the pragmatic demands of fledgling authors who enter the publishing world without the benefit of a Masters in Fine Art and who have to balance their literary pursuits, family, and an existing career.

So you may ask, who am I?

I wrote my first short story when I was sixteen, and I knew in that moment writing would be my creative passion. Pragmatism guided me toward a more stable career path in healthcare, yet I never stopped writing. I didn't have the benefit of creative writing courses, so I studied every book I read to discern the shape and sound of different literary forms. After years of accumulating finished stories, books, and several half-hearted attempts to secure an agent, I decided to approach publication with the discipline of a part-time job. I devoted a certain number of hours each week to submissions, proofreading, and publication research. Several months later I had my first publication credit.

Since then I've gone on to publish fourteen short stories and, to date, three multi-award-winning anthologies. *Remnant*, my first book, combined speculative fiction and science fiction. My second book, *Oddities & Entities*, bridged the supernatural, paranormal, and horror genres. My third book, *Prism*, combined my award-winning, previously published short fiction and new, unpublished pieces to span a wide array of genres and narrative forms. In addition to those three titles, there is this primer and, looking forward, several more completed fiction books that I'm preparing for publication.

One of the interesting things about hindsight is that it makes things sound easy. When I consider that I can sum up what I've done over eight years into two little paragraphs, it makes me wonder why it took so much work to get where I am today. This holds true for any author's story because nobody likes to talk about the labor required for any measure of success in the publishing world. A common thread to every author's story is a long path of hard work and diligent research, two ingredients that don't have much public appeal in the recipe of success. "Success," however, is a word with as many definitions as there are authors who claim its label.

Before my first book came out, I built my website to establish a central presence for my publishing pursuits. Authors are always encouraged to have something on their websites to distinguish them from the crowd, so the course I followed was to include something I hadn't seen on other author sites: essays on lessons learned from someone coming into publishing from the outside. Inspiration struck, so I added a page to my website called "For the Writer". I continue to maintain the page as an evolving source of information.

This book grew from those essays, allowing me to cover not only more topics but also cover them in greater depth. Specifically, Part I concerns the literary craft, Part II explores basic writing mechanics, Part III looks into short story publication, Part IV looks into the world of book publication, and Part V concerns marketing. Some of these sections inevitably overlap, but that's the nature of the beast.

Certain keywords will come up again and again in the course of these discussions. Perseverance, patience, and discipline are essential elements any writer must possess. The market can be unforgiving and, at times, downright brutal. It will test your resolve and your sensitivities to their very limits. Despite these characteristics—or perhaps *because* of them—the publishing world can also provide an unparalleled sense of accomplishment.

One of the little analogies I like to share with people is to imagine sitting in a room among a crowd of strangers. Now imagine that someone takes the stage and asks for a show of hands for a series of questions. Who has written a short story? Who has written a book? Who has been published? Published twice? More than twice? Won an award? Won two awards? Done an interview? Sat at a book signing?

Now ask yourself: how many times do you want to raise your hand?

PART I

Regarding the Literary Craft

"Okay, I have an idea for a story, so I guess I'll take a crack at being an author. What am I getting myself into?"

PERHAPS THE MOST INTERESTING PART of that question is the question itself. Most people don't consider what it means to be an author or what publication entails until after they've finished their first written piece. Either way, there are certain fundamental realities to keep in mind when entering the publishing world. In this section we'll take a look at those realities.

- A brief introduction to the publishing world
- It's never too late to start a publishing adventure
- How to develop a publishing strategy
- The necessity of perseverance and patience
- The necessity of time structure and time discipline
- Realistic expectations and the "overnight sensation" myth
- Join a local authors group
- Economic and expense considerations
- Research, research, and more research
- Train your creativity: write all you can
- Copyright: how it protects an author's work

A brief introduction to the publishing world

TO PARAPHRASE AN OLD SAYING, there's a good book in every person.

In the modern publishing world, this statement is just as valid as in the past, and at the same time it represents an accomplishment one can attain with greater ease. This also holds true for the short story market.

In today's world the only impediment to achieving publication in any form is one's ability to persevere.

For the first-time author, or the author seeking a first publication credit, the publishing world can be intimidating. In the old days of publishing, there were print journals and magazines for short stories and a relatively narrow range of book publishers to query. The advent of the Internet has changed everything. While there has certainly been a contraction of print outlets for the short story market, there's been a corresponding explosion of outlets in the online world. This holds true in the book market as well. Although the profitability of major publishers has been hotly debated in recent years, and the top level of the publishing market has seen various mergers and acquisitions, the book market has nevertheless seen an overall growth in opportunities for authors to get their writings published.

In the old days the only outlet for published material was print. While it may seem obvious that the Internet has changed that situation, the depth of that change is not readily apparent to all those who venture into publishing. In the early days of the Internet, journals were divided between print and electronic formats. Contractions in the print market and growth in the electronic market have blurred those lines so that many journals print in multiple formats—print, electronic, and yes, audio. The audio market is still in its early stages, but it's a direct descendant of the electronic market, and for some creative presentations it can offer an outlet that didn't previously exist.

By the same token the book market of old was divided among major, small, and so-called "vanity" publishers. The borders between these three models were clearly defined and represented career benchmarks for some authors. The publishing world of today has seen a marked blurring of those delineations, in part due to the proliferation of e-books. As with journals, there's no clear border between publishers who specialize in one format or another; in fact, no such border exists. The competition within the book market has compelled almost all publishers to employ multiple formats. By the same token, the presence of online outlets such as Amazon and the electronic extension of Barnes & Noble enables publishers of all scale, and their authors, to get equal share on virtual bookshelves.

There will be more specific discussion on publisher segments in succeeding sections, particularly in Part 4, Regarding Novels. For now suffice it to say that the Internet has led to a vast grass roots expansion of publishing opportunities. While this has made publication a somewhat easier goal to attain, the sheer mass of published material has made the tricky task of getting noticed all the more difficult.

It's never too late to start a publishing adventure

ONE OF THE FASCINATING ELEMENTS of the publishing world is the incredible diversity of authors. There are the obvious differences in what material authors create, but beyond that surface variation, one will also find just as rich a variety in authors' personal backgrounds. The beauty of being an author is that it's never too late to begin. It's common for published authors to wish they started earlier in their pursuit; at the same time they concede that in those earlier days they weren't in a proper life moment to pursue their goal.

This is something to which I can personally attest. I started writing when I was sixteen. My earliest forms of creative expression involved art. As I grew I desired to depict situations too complex for a single picture to convey. Reading was my main hobby and I devoured books to feed my intellectual and artistic curiosity. It didn't take long before I found myself questioning how plots could change if the author went in a different direction, and this growing form of critique and analysis culminated in a natural deduction: I should write a story of my own. The moment I put the final period on that first draft, I knew that writing would be my creative outlet.

Life was a different matter however. Even though I was compelled to write, I had a very pragmatic set of goals through college and into my early adulthood that demanded a stable financial picture. Living on the crumbs of a fledgling publishing dream simply wasn't acceptable. As the years rolled by, I had nothing to show for all my desire except a dream that was becoming more a source of frustration than anything else.

In 2007 I changed my strategy. I decided the time of complaining about not being published had to end, and this is where I aim to illustrate my point. My years of creativity provided me with a stable of short stories and books. They all needed serious editing and revision, but I had ample raw material in hand. Also, being a little older, I had the maturity to properly discipline myself for the efforts that publication would require. Last but not least I had a plan rather than sending out something here and there with little more than an abstract hope.

Moving forward to where I am now, I can see how everything fit together. The caliber of stories I used for publication was yet to exist within me, and I lacked the discipline to keep pounding away in the effort to get published.

In hindsight I believe things happened in the only temporal order possible to put my writing career where it is today. The moral of the story is that publication is a personal and professional process that has to develop at its own pace.

How to develop a publishing strategy

THE BEST STORY IN THE world won't amount to much if it never finds its way into the hands of readers. How an author seeks to realize this process will depend on many factors, and there are probably just as many options. Nevertheless, there are a few common-sense strategies based on an initial concept of what you want from your pursuits as an author and your writing experience.

Let's start with a somewhat semantic question: do you want to be a writer or an author? A *writer* is someone who was compelled to put one story into words. Life is an incredibly diverse experience among individuals, providing people with singular interpretations of existence that can translate into unique written expression, whether it takes the form of non-fiction or fiction. However, some people have more than one book in mind. *Authors* form this second group of people.

For authors the act of creating stories is a perpetual pursuit. While writers can earn a well-deserved sense of accomplishment by seeing a single book through to publication, authors are always eager to start their next book. Writers create a book to satisfy a desire, whereas authors move to new books because they have a restless sense of creativity pushing them to summon something new. Authors are compelled to write.

Why is this an important difference to understand? Upon entering the world of book publishing, there are many options available. Some of them are more suited to those who have an interest in presenting a single book, while other options are more suitable for those who are looking for a sustained output of titles. This will be discussed in more detail in Part 4, Regarding Novels. For now it's something to keep in mind when considering what path to take for one's publishing future.

It's important to note that these definitions are not binding. I've met quite a few authors who thought they were interested in doing just one book. After experiencing the process of seeing a single book through to publication, they were bitten by the writer's bug and couldn't wait to start another book. For those who are ready to invest themselves in their work, I think every writer has an author waiting inside.

The separation between pursuing a single book and building a writing career will be most apparent in the way one approaches the publication world. For those who have a single book, their road will lead straight to concerns for book publishing. These aspiring individuals will have to choose among self-, small-, or large publishers and whether or not to court a literary agent for representation. If the goal is to land with a large publisher, an agent is a must. After the initial decision of what level of publisher to pursue, all other concerns will be toward marketing.

Those who wish to build a career as an author have more considerations at hand. To start, building a career as an author is no different than building any other career in that it's perhaps best to start small and build up through successive steps. The short story market is a great place for career-minded authors to settle into the realities of the publishing world and to hone their narrative skills. A growing list of publication credits can also be a vital step toward wooing an agent or publisher, in addition to building confidence. This is exactly the strategy I used to break into publishing.

Book publication is the inevitable next step from the world of short stories. At that point, hopefully, an author will have collected a sufficient body of publishing and market knowledge to ensure sound decisions. Even so, authors will join their writing brethren in having to choose whether or not to court a literary agent and what scale of publisher to pursue.

The necessity of perseverance and patience

I'VE BEEN ASKED ON NUMEROUS occasions what would be the best piece of advice for aspiring authors. In the past I've used the word *persistence*, but I'm going to change that word to *perseverance* to create more positive spin. Even though patience is built into perseverance, it's so important that I like to list it on its own.

The reality of the publishing world is that authors spend immense amounts of time on efforts that go unnoticed. There's the obvious time investment in writing, editing, proofing, and revision. What escapes common perception, however, is the time consumed by researching submission targets, marketing strategies, and general education on the publishing world.

I'm going to paraphrase a telling statistic: the average short story endures forty rejected submission queries and two years of query wait times before being accepted for publication. The average short story is 5,000 words in length. By rough estimate even a meticulous reader should be able to digest a story of that length in a brief sitting. Looking at that time imbalance, it's quite clear that there's a huge investment of effort in comparison to the actual dividend.

This isn't meant to discourage. In fact the intention is the exact opposite. Too many authors give up when they run face first into a wall of rejection. For these authors, rejection constitutes the most prominent characteristic of the publishing world because they have the misconception that attaining publication is a quick and easy process. For those who aren't concerned with the quality of their work—or where it appears—the process can indeed be quick and easy, yet the end product will be of questionable value.

To attain writing credits of which one can be proud entails confronting a publishing world that is at once fiercely competitive and highly subjective. If the best story in the world doesn't fall within a particular editor's tastes, it will find its way to the rejection pile. The message to hold near and dear is that almost every written piece will require multiple submissions and the associated time to find its home in a market. Knowing this beforehand can do much to allay the anxiety of rejections.

The book world is no different. There are numerous stories of A-list authors who, as unknowns, had their first novels rejected by seventy or more literary agencies. Of those who at last secured their agent and publication, few had immediate sales success. It often takes several titles before an author can establish any footprint within the publishing world. I've read in several columns that the average author should expect to publish five or six books before enjoying any sales momentum. Whether one pursues the traditional route of agent representation or independent publishing, be prepared for an up-hill battle when it comes to marketing.

The wonder of the Internet is that it puts every book on equal footing out of the publication gate. Authors with prominent names and major publishers appear on Amazon alongside unknowns with small or self-publishers. The problem with the Internet is that the popularization of the publishing process allows so many titles to see publication that it's very easy to be lost in the crowd. Prominent authors already have the name recognition that helps buoy them above the masses. For everyone else the struggle to earn recognition and a reader following has just begun.

It won't be an easy path. There will be disappointments, and sometimes the hurdles will seem insurmountable. Painful amounts of time may pass with the impression that there's little or nothing to show for the temporal and emotional investment. The temptation to despair in the face of futility will be great.

In these times it's important to remember one simple thing: hundreds of thousands of titles reach print every year, but only a tiny percentage will achieve anything beyond their actual publication. The difference lies in the perseverance of the author. When confronted with the stark reality of the publishing world, too many people simply resign from the effort to champion their books. They look at publication as an aspiration now accomplished or an item to be crossed off on a bucket-list. For the serious author, publication is the first public step in what will be an ongoing process.

The necessity of time structure and time discipline

VERY FEW PEOPLE CAN PURSUE their writing aspirations without having to concern themselves with the pragmatic reality of financial security. Likewise, there are few who have enough financial security to support open-ended expenses for their aspirations. There are authors who work to support themselves—and their families—in addition to their lives as authors, there are authors who no longer work but who have other obligations that consume their time, and there are authors who spread themselves too thin to focus on any one particular effort. While every author will come to the publishing table with his or her own private story, the one thing every author has in common is the challenge of time management.

The most common pitfall of time management is to read too much advice on this very subject. Yes, it is somewhat ironic. The problem with most so-called "advice" pieces for authors is that they don't really add up to realistic plans. Most of these discourses stress that authors should spend a certain amount of time every day on a number of social networks—Facebook, Twitter, etc.—a certain amount of time writing and proofing, a certain amount of time on marketing, and a certain amount of time reading and researching top-selling books within an author's area of interest.

Although there are variances from plan to plan, on average these plans consist of time allotments that don't fit the typical day of an author. Specifically, they all too often neglect time for a job that provides the author and his/her family with food and shelter, time to spend with one's family, and let's not forget time to sleep. After twenty-five years of working midnight shifts, sleep scheduling is something near and dear to me.

I believe the best advice on this topic is to take a close look at your average life schedule over a week or two, and use a pragmatic approach to how many hours can be devoted to your publishing pursuits. There's no avoiding a time investment in your efforts. For years I approached publication with half-hearted pursuits. I said earlier I would send out a few agent queries and then move on to a new project. In short that was the wrong plan. I will once again use the word perseverance, because one of the motivational killers for aspiring authors is the time demand embodied by publication pursuits.

Consider publication as a part-time job. By assuming this frame of thought, you at once understand that you have to find at least a few hours a week to dedicate to your efforts. If there's more time, great; if there's less, then find a way to make up those lost hours. The advantage to this approach is that it builds the sense of routine into your pursuit. Once you succeed at disciplining yourself to the necessary time allotment, it won't feel like something extra. After all, humans are creatures of habit.

Remember that realizing publication should be an author's passion. If you find yourself resistant to making those time commitments, then you need to change your approach to what you do in that time. On occasion it can be monotonous and seem futile, but keep the end goal in sight. Another good way to make your time more productive and seem less like work is to mix your tasks. When you sit down to invest your time, consider what you need to do in that time and what you feel motivated to do in that time. A healthy balance will make your time allotment more productive and entrench a fundamental aspect of your efforts: you should be having *fun* as an author.

Realistic expectations and the "overnight sensation" myth

THE POPULAR MYTH OF THE publishing world is that publication instantly translates to large financial returns. This fallacy is typified in the story that a previously unknown author just landed a six-figure publishing deal with a major publishing house on a first book, and movie rights are already sold for development.

For all the other authors—99.99%, at least—who sit and patiently send out submissions, sift through edits and revisions, and understand that the business of writing is one laden with patience, that tired blurb is a painful pill to swallow. Such accounts are only noteworthy if they illuminate how the author in question managed to secure the kind of unique attention leading to such rapid success. By comparison, for every

Hollywood sensation that gets "discovered" standing outside a club, there's a horde of struggling actors who go to acting school and pursue the endless exercise of auditions. The same can be said for the music industry.

These blurbs exist because they touch upon something to which we can all relate. It's the fantasy of quick and easy success, also known as the lottery mentality. In most cases it's just that, a fantasy. A study of successful people in any creative medium most often reveals a far more realistic story in which success manifests after years of hard work developing the respective and requisite skills.

Earlier on I paraphrased a set of statistics, but it's useful to repeat them here. The typical short story endures forty rejections and two years of submissions before publication; the average author/book endures seventy or more agent rejections before being signed—and then the book has to be picked up by a publisher.

Remember that "success" has many incarnations. Your first publication credit is a huge success because no matter how far you want to go, you're nowhere without that first step. A second credit, that's great, because now you know you're not a "one-hit" deal. A third can build some legitimate confidence. A fourth and you start to feel like part of the publishing world.

Join a local authors group

DEPENDING ON THE AREA IN which you live, there may be a number of author groups for you to join. I cannot stress enough the importance of taking this step.

For fledgling authors it can be very difficult to gain inroads with local venues such as bookstores or schools, much less justify the cost burden of table fees at fairs or book signing events. A local author group provides strength in numbers as well as mutual support. Until you achieve name recognition as an author, it's very difficult to draw a crowd to an event or recoup an appearance fee through book sales. The combined self-publicity of fellow authors, as well as a group's promotional efforts, can help overcome these hurdles. In addition, the support of a group can divide the time-consuming efforts to set up events and appearances, as well as bring in potential contacts through other authors in the group. Perhaps of most importance though is the great sense of camaraderie you can experience by meeting other authors.

Writing by its very nature is a solitary pursuit. Aside from the obvious time spent researching, writing, editing, and revising a manuscript, there are many hours of research involved after a book is published. The Internet has been a great facilitator for both publication and marketing efforts from the comfort of your own desk. However, at the same time it also serves as a great isolator as you toil in what can seem like a claustrophobic vacuum. Meeting other authors lets you realize that your struggles and triumphs are not alone, while allowing you to share ideas and beliefs about writing and publishing. You'll also have the opportunity to learn about ideas or opportunities that escaped your perception.

Author groups provide a social forum for people who share in the reality of publishing. Authors form an incredibly imaginative and interesting culture of their own, and a group provides the opportunity to meet people from many walks of life with different ideological backgrounds. It's essential for authors to understand the humanity in people and to be open-minded enough to listen to varying experiences and viewpoints. After all, the most fundamental part of good storytelling is the vibrancy of your characters. If you can't open yourself up to other creative people, you do a great disservice to your own creative potential.

Economic and expense considerations

ALTHOUGH THE INITIAL PROCESS OF writing is a "free" expenditure from the resources of your imagination, publication will require real world monetary investment.

Given the slow-building trend of a publication pursuit, it's quite easy to lose track of your expenses. This can be magnified by the idea that pursuing publication is a dream, so the financial consideration can be secondary to manifesting a long-held ambition. Nevertheless, as with any other financial engagement, numbers are unforgiving.

For those working in the short story market, costs are negligible. Aside from the bare material necessities an author requires—such as some type of computer, an Internet connection, and perhaps some notepads—there's little additional expense. Most publications accept electronic submissions, thereby eliminating postal expenses, and the few publications that charge submission fees often leverage their fee against the cost of a postal submission. While this is good news, the not-so-good news is that there's very little money to be made in the short story market. There are some well-paying professional publications that offer several hundred dollars for a single story, but these publications are both extremely selective and form a remote percentage of available publications. The vast majority of short story publications do not pay for printed stories; the main reward for the author is the publication credit.

For those entering the book market, things are quite different. Depending on the type of publisher one works with, there may be an up-front book production cost. With self-publishers this figure can run in the neighborhood of a thousand dollars or more, depending on the publication package selected. Outside of the self-publishing route, there may also be independent editorial costs to absorb prior to publication if the author sought professional help in refining a manuscript.

After publication the biggest cost—and biggest investment risk—is marketing. Depending on what one chooses to do, this aspect of a book's financial life can be bottomless. Professional reviews, contest entries, advertising, virtual book tours, press packages, press releases, and so forth, all have associated costs that can quickly add up to thousands of dollars with no guarantees of compensation through sales income.

How much one can be spend will of course be unique to each author's financial resources and derived income. It's crucial to understand, however, that without some type of promotion investment, a book will most likely flounder. Social networking is often considered "free" in terms of monetary expense, yet it requires a steep time investment for any hope of success.

While there's no way to avoid costs as an author, there are ways to abate those costs. The first step is the most basic and so the easiest to overlook: invest with your head, not your heart. There's always an associated risk to investing in a book, and no reputable marketing or promotional service will ever guarantee a sales return. Until book sales can buoy book costs, the costs will unfortunately be supported by existing income. It's important to believe in your book, but don't be blinded by confidence.

The second step is to try to invest in things that offer solid returns outside of book sales. Reviews and awards, in themselves, do not guarantee sales, but they do provide return dividends in credentials and critique quotes that will comprise your promotional presence.

The third step is somewhat more complicated. For those serious about their book efforts, whether it's the plan to publish several books or heavily promote a single title, there should be serious consideration to incorporate as either an S-corp or LLC. Tax laws vary from state to state, and it's best to consult a tax professional before taking any steps, but incorporation can provide significant tax benefits, both in deductions for expenses and lower tax rates on publication income. It will require some additional paperwork to maintain the business, along with the expense of a postal box and a business bank account, but moving forward, this step can be a valuable economic resource.

Another vital advantage of incorporating is that you will obtain a state sales tax certificate. Why is this important? Some events, such as fairs, require proof of your state sales tax certificate to cover their own compliance under state sales tax law. This will enable them to transfer responsibility for sales tax payment from the fair organizers to the individual retailers—such as an author selling books—at the fair. Without this piece of documentation, such appearances won't be possible.

Incorporating isn't difficult or expensive. Online legal services such as Legal Zoom offer incorporation options. Accountants and lawyers can offer these services as well, though their price may exceed the do-it-yourself options.

We will revisit economic concerns for your publishing pursuits in later parts of this book.

Research, research, and more research

THERE'S A SAYING IN THE world of real estate that the three most important characteristics of a particular site are location, location, location. For an author three of the most important parts of a publication pursuit are research, research, and more research.

There are two phases of research required upon entering the publishing world. One phase is the research an author employs in building a knowledge base for writing a particular story or book. Authors often discuss this effort to lend credibility to the work in question. The second phase of research is one authors are less inclined to discuss, and that's research regarding the publishing world itself.

The reason for this is rather simple. While learning about the publishing world can unlock some of the doors of knowledge, the process can consume a great deal of time and not always produce something of direct value. In short, research can be tedious. Nevertheless, it's essential.

Many authors get lost in the marketplace because they fail to properly prepare themselves for each phase of their writing endeavor. The research that may be required to write a certain piece isn't looked upon as labor, because it's woven into the excitement of crafting the work in question. Research to find a suitable publication outlet is again wrapped up in the overall excitement of bringing a piece to life, yet here waits the first opportunity to stumble. Receiving a publication acceptance can be a seductive thrill, but it's important for an author to understand as much as possible about the publisher before entering any agreements. The truth of the matter is the author should learn everything possible about a publisher, agent, or editor *before* submitting any work. Ask yourself ahead of time if you're ready, without reservation, to engage in a business relationship with a given entity before you submit.

After publication the requirement of research doesn't go away. The publishing world is a rapidly changing environment, and the momentous changes brought to this environment through the Internet, self-publishing, and e-books have unsettled long-established equilibriums. It's impossible to know everything about the landscape in which authors pursue their literary aspirations, but as an individual author it's vital to learn as much as possible. At the least, as a fledgling author, you want to know enough of the publishing world to recognize something that might be of benefit so that you can then focus your attention. This is particularly true of marketing and promotion.

In the prior section regarding local author groups, I mentioned the ability to share knowledge within a group. Given the depth of options in the publishing world, in a room full of authors, every author will probably be aware of something that has escaped the others. This pool of collective information can illuminate possibilities an individual author had not seen, and also serve as a reminder that research is an endless process.

In the publication world there are three truths: there are those who know more, there are those who have more resources, and there are those fortunate to have both these advantages. Your personal knowledge base is the best way to level the playing field.

Train your creativity: write all you can

JUST LIKE AN ATHLETE TRAINING to compete, as an author you have to hone your creative skills through the experience of writing. In the simplest of terms, there's no replacement for the act of writing, itself. It may sound obvious that authors have to write, but the intention is to understand that not every written word will go somewhere, and not every written word need serve a specific purpose.

There are many pundits and advice columns that suggest authors write at least one to two thousand words a day. It's a wonderful idea, but it's not that realistic in the context of those who already have jobs and families as time priorities in their lives. Nevertheless, at least part of an author's creative energy should be devoted to the mechanical process of writing. If there's no time to put sentences to paper or keyboard, at least try to formulate passages in your head. The best ideas in the world go nowhere if the person who holds them can't effectively translate them to marketable prose.

Many creative writing programs and how-to books suggest batteries of writing exercises. While the formality of such exercises will vary by their source, even those who are considering writing from the most casual reference frame can benefit from this pursuit. There's much to learn from simply writing a descriptive passage of what you saw on your way to work or in writing a dialog between two people.

The most important part of writing exercises is to understand that the point of an exercise is to develop the translation from raw creativity to written word rather than creating a definitive story. Look at what you wrote and compare it to the creative inspiration that drove the words into being. Do they fit the mood you wanted? Do they convey the meaning you desired? Do grammar issues get in the way of what you wanted to show in your writing? These are but a few of the questions to examine when both writing and revisiting such creative experimentation.

As you move forward with your writing, you'll notice an increasing tendency to reference an automatic editor in your head who will instinctually guide you away from basic, common, and fundamental errors. The development of an intrinsic self-editor will ease the writing process, but it only comes from practice.

Nevertheless, your first writing endeavors will most likely require extensive revision, editing, or even a complete rewrite. These are all valuable lessons for learning and shouldn't be confused as an argument that writing is too difficult to successfully complete a story. Many authors, even established authors, will admit embarrassment over the first stories they put to paper. Ask authors about their writing and you'll hear one thing over and over. Every author knows the desire to go back and fix a passage, revise wording, or wish the voice within a given piece could've been more focused.

The learning process may be endless, but the good news is that it starts with the first words you write.

Copyright: how it protects an author's work

Anyone considering publication needs to have a working understanding of copyright law.

Copyright law is an internationally recognized standard of legal rights for content creators, wherein *content* is defined as a unique creative product. In essence the moment content is created and the creator attaches his or her name, copyright law goes into effect. The law protects the existing form of a created work. For authors this somewhat nebulous phrase contains a subtle but important consideration: copyright law *does* protect the specific expression of a work; it *does not* protect the ideas expressed in the work. For example one cannot copyright the concept of a murder mystery in which a wife kills her cheating husband. However, copyright *will* protect the specific content of a particular work, so a murder mystery where a wife kills her husband can have its unique wording and characters safeguarded.

As a side note be mindful that copyright is an *international standard*. Among signatory nations to the standard, the applicable protections of the enacted law are relatively consistent. However, not all nations have signed onto the law. North Korea is most notable, but for all realistic purposes most authors aren't looking to break down the door of the North Korean publishing market.

On the other hand there are nations of questionable status. Microsoft, for example, has a decided opinion about certain nations' respect—or lack thereof—for copyright law. It's a big reason for the move to licensed subscription software from not just Microsoft but many other major software companies. The publishing world has seen its problems as well. Some foreign publishing markets are judged to have huge growth potential, which creates the dilemma of how to participate in those markets with copyright assurance. Authors need to be wary of independently submitting their work to any foreign publishers. For authors considering foreign publication, the safest course is to let a domestic publisher or agent manage such an interaction.

Copyright law provides a very simple mechanism to enact protection. On a written work, the author need only follow the title with the word *copyright* or the abbreviation *copyr.*, the year of creation, and the author's name. Among publication professionals the accepted standard is the author's name and year of creation; indeed, there are quite a few editors of short story publications who consider it a personal offense—and the sign of an unprofessional amateur—when the author spells out or abbreviates the word copyright.

How does copyright factor into the publication process? When an author creates a written work, the author is immediately in ownership of all rights to represent that work in any form. To publish the work the author sells—monetary exchange—or grants—no monetary exchange—a *right* of the work to the publisher. The exact details will vary with the publication, and some rights can only be exchanged once in the life of a work. For example most short stories are published with the publisher specifying that it will take first serial rights. This means the author allows that publisher the first opportunity to publish the work. Reputable publication agreements will contain a provision for return of right(s) to the author. Returning to the short story example, a publisher may specify exclusivity for a year before rights return to the author, at which point the author is free to publish the story elsewhere.

Every time an author's work is published, there's an exercise of copyright management. This exercise is in fact a legal agreement entered into between author and publisher, and these agreements can span a wide scale of complexity. While some provisions of copyright are self-explanatory, others require a certain amount of legal knowledge to properly negotiate. In either case it's incumbent upon the author to understand what rights are being given to a publisher and at what financial compensation. Remember that some rights, once given, can never be restored, as in the above example of first serial rights.

Any reputable entity will always clearly define the rights claimed in a publication agreement and will specify the return of rights upon the expiration of the agreement. If a publication or publisher is unwilling to have full and open disclosure with an author as to the rights sought, the author should be wary of the agreement or contract. Copyright cases can be extremely complicated and so very expensive to pursue in a court of law.

While authors are understandably protective of their own work, it's important to understand how copyright covers the work of others. The *fair use* clause of copyright allows certain aspects of a copyrighted work to be used in the creative content of others. For authors, this often covers the genre of *fan fiction*, where an author uses existing characters and settings from an established work to create a new story. In technical terms copyright law excludes such usage; however, if the copyright holders of the original content do not object, the usage is allowed. Most often, fan fiction copyright infringement is condoned by the content's original creator(s) because it helps promote the original work. Even so, fair use is a bit of a gray zone, and there are some short story publications that expressly refuse to consider such works in order to avoid copyright allegations and entanglements.

Fair use also covers excerpts of copyrighted material. In the world of research and nonfiction, fair use covers the reference and quoting of previous material, provided the use is properly cited to credit the original author(s). However, fair use does not allow an author to rehash prior copyrighted content as an extensive, intrinsic part of the "new" work, regardless of citation, because the work is not considered new. As long as the author takes the new work in a previously unpublished direction, then again fair use provides coverage.

While fair use is rather unambiguous in the world of nonfiction, it's not quite as clear in the world of fiction. Moving beyond the topic of fan fiction discussed above, this part of fair use bridges the type of usage just discussed in nonfiction. For example, in a work of fiction, it's acceptable for characters to discuss another copyrighted work, as long as the title or creator of the work is referenced and—most importantly—there's no overuse of the specific original content. Unfortunately, *overuse* can be a subjective judgment. As with all things involving copyright, common sense can be the best guide.

Let's take a look at some examples.

Fair use: In a book two characters discuss a scene from *The Terminator*, naming the movie and Arnold Schwarzenegger before reciting the line, "I'll be back."

Questionable use: In a book a character dresses up in a leather coat, puts on black sunglasses, and says, "I'll be back." There's no reference in the book to *The Terminator*. Though none of these individual elements are distinct, their combination is in fact a specific reproduction of an iconic scene from the movie.

Fair use: In a story the narrative describes a party and cites characters singing along to a specific pop song.

Questionable use: In a story the narrative describes a party and puts in quotations the lyrics of a pop song to which the characters sing along. If it's one or two lines of the song, and the original song title and artist are mentioned, fair use will most likely come into effect. If an entire verse of the song is used with or without citing the title and artist, it's unlikely fair use will apply.

The best rule of thumb: consider how you would feel if someone else started using material from something *you* wrote, and what you would consider fair use or abusive use.

Authors also need to be careful of *public domain* material. Under older versions of copyright law, content created before a certain date was basically considered public property and not entitled to copyright protection. This has changed, and continues to change, as the Internet impacts the way copyrighted works are disseminated. Overall, the time span of copyright protection has been expanded.

Public domain material can often be misconstrued as *open source* material and vice versa. Open source material is content where the creators have surrendered their rights so that others can use the material. This is most commonly experienced with pictures on the Internet, which are easily searched with the simple phrase *open source images.*

Translations are another tricky area of copyright law. For example, Homer's *Iliad* itself is not copyright protected. However, a particular translator's version of Homer's *Iliad* is copyright protected because the translation is the singular work of that particular author. The text within the translation can only be used with the permission of the translator. Conversely, the translator need not seek permission since the original Greek form of the *Iliad* is not protected.

Regardless of the situation, if an author uses any content from an external source, it's the author's legal responsibility to determine if permission is required from the creator of said work. A common source of error, and a common source of restriction in recent years, is the quoting of lyrics in written works. Song titles, album titles, and the names of performers are not copyright restricted, but the lyrics are most definitely copyright protected. In fact many editors will flat out refuse to look at material—particularly short stories—containing lyrics from songs the author did not personally create.

As a final note, an author's name, character names, and book titles do not fall under copyright protection. Names and titles fall under the domain of trademark law rather than copyright law, which is a completely separate legal topic.

To reiterate, the best guide to copyright law, as with most things, is to use common sense. It doesn't take much insight to understand when one crosses the line in the use of existing material. Considering the fallout of copyright violation, it's not worth the risk. While plagiarism is a black eye in the academic world, it's a stake through the heart in the publishing world. Even an accusation of plagiarism can forever mar an author's reputation. When in doubt, contact the original copyright holder before using any material.

PART 2

Basic Writing Mechanics

*"Well, I started writing my story, and my word processor lit up with all these
red and green underlines. Why does my writing look more like a Christmas
decoration than a story?"*

IN AN EFFORT TO SOLVE this dilemma, we'll take a look at the
following topics:

- Basic writing mechanics: are you ready to submit?
- Point of view: differentiating 1st, 2nd, and 3rd person narrative
- Characterization: summoning life within a story
- Writing dialog: giving characters their voice
- Plotting: getting from beginning to end
- Setting: story environment and world building
- Levels of editing: copy edit, line edit, and content edit
- When enough is enough: working with explicit content
- Developing your narrative voice

Of the many people who aspire to publication, only a handful benefit
from a formal education in the literary arts. For everyone else the notion
of jumping into the publishing world without a degree in creative writing
or literature can be a discouraging prospect.

There's no need to despair. Yes, the learning curve will be somewhat
steeper than for those with a formal education in the craft of writing;
and yes, for those who lack that background, it's imperative to learn
everything possible to catch the appreciative eye of an editor or agent.
Regardless of how compelling a character or how fantastic the plot of
a particular story, the writing must meet market expectation to find a
respectable home. Authors should always maintain the perspective that
an author is a manufacturer and writing is the author's product. As with

any other endeavor, products that lack quality won't find a lasting presence in the marketplace.

Poorly written manuscripts are an unfortunate part of the publishing world due to the less-than-discriminating standards of some publishers and publications. While a rare few of these pieces may find commercial success, the stark reality is that the vast majority of these works serve little more than to clutter the literary landscape and thereby increase the difficulty for creditable works to gain recognition. It's a harsh statement, but it accurately reflects the unforgiving nature of the publishing world.

If there's one piece of concrete advice to offer, it's to buy a paperback-sized combination dictionary/thesaurus and keep it near whenever you write. Not only will it prevent word misuse, it allows you to expand your vocabulary and prevent your word usage from stagnating.

So, like me, you may be entering the publishing world without the benefit of a formal education in the literary arts. You ain't got nothin' to worry 'bout. The following sections are meant to elicit awareness for the most fundamental element of an author's craft, the writing itself.

Basic writing mechanics: are you ready to submit?

Make no mistake about pursuing publication in any form or length: if you want to succeed, you must understand basic principles of grammar. It's far too easy for prospective authors to see their work sabotaged by failing to properly prepare their manuscripts. The evidence of this problem is clear in the submission instructions of countless short story markets where editors are confronted with a large draw of aspiring authors.

This isn't to say that you need to earn a doctorate in grammar before sending out material. Even a small foray through editorial advice columns will reveal a simple truth that too many novice authors overlook. Regardless of how passionate a novice can be regarding publication, it's important to understand that while writing may be a hobby for the novice in many cases, it's the business—or even livelihood—of the submission target. Submissions should be approached with no less attention to professional detail than a resume for a job application because in many ways querying for publication is in fact applying for a job.

It's unfortunate that in today's world grammar no longer receives the attention in primary and secondary school settings it once did. For most people this is perhaps of negligible concern. On the other hand, for those who seek publication, it can pose a problem. Editors expect submitted work to display a working knowledge of grammar; at the same time, editors are not responsible for teaching grammar. Although in many cases this is an unspoken reality, many editors still do take the time to remind people of this point. A story or novel could contain the best idea in literary history only to be rejected if an editor or review reader can't make it through the first page—or even the first paragraph—without stumbling over numerous examples of faulty grammar.

So how does one overcome this issue? There are two simple approaches. The first is the obvious: go out and buy a grammar guide at a bookstore. The second approach can't be emphasized enough: study books that have been published. By analyzing the form and structure of writing in published books, it's not difficult to discern both proper writing mechanics and market-acceptable narrative standards. This was the approach I used to tackle the grammar problem, and while my experience is singular to me, there isn't an advice column or author out there who won't stress the importance of reading other published books.

A manuscript should be in the best grammar form possible. With that said, there's no such thing as a perfect manuscript. When it comes to short stories, most editors won't invest the effort to do an editorial review on a submitted piece before publication because they simply don't have the time and manpower to extend such effort. The submission will be accepted—or rejected—on its face. In some select short story publications, and with any reputable book publisher, editorial exchange will occur before a piece goes to publication in its final form. In these cases, authors who refuse to take editorial advice can quickly find their work transferred from publication path to rejection pile. Blank refusal of editorial input is a blatant sign an author isn't ready to professionally approach publication.

Here's a very simple checklist to review for those who are first entering the publication process.

Initial Checklist:

1. At the least use Spell/Grammar check in your word processor—the red and green lines in your document are not the aforementioned Christmas decorations; they're issues that need to be addressed.
2. Remember your usage of punctuation.
3. That said, remember the comma is to list items, separate ideas, link action, or lead into/out of dialog. (He said, "Go to the store." / "I will," I said.)
4. The period is a wonderful thing, but don't abuse ellipses, those three periods that indicate a trailing, incomplete thought or sentence, so ... a few of these can be used for dramatic purpose; otherwise, they say to an editor that the author didn't know how to end the narrative passage.
5. Understand the semi-colon; the semi-colon is used to link related but independent ideas or statements, as was just done.
6. Consider that in most cases in which you might use a semi-colon, you can probably create two independent sentences that have better narrative flow. Semi-colons are more acceptable in nonfiction than fiction.
7. If you're writing fiction, it's unlikely to have any valid use or place for a colon.
8. Make sure of proper use between *to, too,* and *two*:

    to indicates a transfer or movement: go *to* the store and give money *to* the clerk;

    too indicates something in addition, think *also*: I bought some ice cream and a shovel, *too;*

    too can also indicate an extended measure: I put *too* much ice cream on my shovel;

    two ...well, it's just a number ...
9. Make sure of proper use of *your* and *you're*:

    your as in the possessive form of *you*: that's *your* shovel;

    you're as in the contraction of *you are*: if you swing that shovel *you're* in trouble.

10. And don't forget the difference between *there, their,* and *they're:*
    > *there* as in a physical or abstract location: I'm going over *there* with my shovel;
    >
    > *their* as in the possessive of individuals: that's *their* playing field I'm digging up;
    >
    > *they're* as in the contraction of *they are; they're* after me now that I dug up the field.

11. While you're at it, don't forget the difference between *its* and *it's:*
    > *its* is the possessive form of *it:* while digging up the field I was drenched by *its* sprinklers;
    >
    > *it's* is the contraction of *it is:* those sprinklers throw so much water you'd think *it's* raining.

    Misuse and confusion between *its* and *it's* are perhaps the most common grammatical miscues seen when people write. If you want to be an author, don't be one of those people.

12. Why is it so important to remember the differences between these words? One simple answer: spell-check tools in word processors may fail to detect improper usage among these words.

13. Once you've gone over all of that, you might as well go back and do another proofread, just to be sure.

✸

AT THIS POINT OF THE process, it's a good idea to pay close attention to comma and period usage beyond strict grammatical concerns. In classical literature it was accepted narrative practice to use long flowing sentences with their internal structure linked by commas. Modern literary practice has moved away from that and favors shorter, more concise sentences. Failure to adhere to this more "modern" style runs the risk of giving the narrative a rather dated sound.

The easiest and perhaps best way to ensure the proper flow of sentences with their commas and periods is to read them aloud. Don't forget that no matter what you may know—or not know—of grammar rules, commas and periods are intrinsic cues to the mind of a reader. Without deviating into the neurological aspect of reading, suffice it to say, a reader's mind responds to commas and periods in a way we as authors may overlook because we know our intended meaning while the reader does not. By reading aloud, this issue is removed and the author can hear the sentence flow in the same manner as a reader.

Commas are instinctual cues for a pause within a sentence, alerting the reader that an additional statement aside from the initial intent of the sentence will be forthcoming. Periods are like little reset buttons that alert a reader to a new phase of the narrative. Periods also cue a pause. If, while reading aloud, you find your narrative laced with pauses, then your sentences need to be reorganized to achieve a more even flow. If you get lost in the pauses of commas, or the interruption of the original sentence led you too far astray, the sentence most likely needs to be separated into two or more passages.

A good way to get a sense of proper narrative flow, particularly for beginning authors, is to obtain a well-reviewed book and read it aloud. If this is done in comparison to your own writing, it's much easier to hear the difference between polished narrative flow and less polished flow.

Some beginning authors make the mistake of believing that their writing should reflect the sound of their thoughts. The answer to this is yes and no. Yes, every author should strive to develop a unique narrative voice; this will help distinguish the author's writing. On the other hand, narrative structure has to be in a form that's accessible. Readers shouldn't have to guess what an author is trying to say.

Speaking of style, a stylistic issue in fiction that's often debated is the use of adverbs. To be clear, adverbs—often but not always identified by the -ly suffix—are used to describe the actions of verbs, adjectives, and other adverbs, as in "he ran quickly," "she snored loudly," or "it was much earlier than I thought." Some authors and critics take the strict stance that fiction prose should never contain adverbs, while others recommend they should be avoided but not shunned. Criticism of adverb use stems from the belief that adverbs are, in effect, lazy ways to describe action within a narrative. As an extension of this judgment, they are even considered to violate the border between *telling* and *showing* a story, which is to say, whether or not a narrative reads like a lab report or exists as a living entity within a reader's mind.

Regardless of anyone's view on the use of adverbs, there's no denying that a narrative avoiding adverbs is more captivating than a narrative that relies on their usage. A simple exercise is to write passages both with and without adverbs and then see in comparison how vivid descriptive passages become without adverbs. In addition, most adverbs have a very distinct *lee* sound from the -ly suffix, and even sparse use creates a disruptive *lee, lee, lee* intonation to the narrative.

Consider the following passage:

> *Pete quickly ran to the store, rapidly running out of breath as his legs steadily strained.*

Now consider a revision without adverbs:

> *Pete ran to the store as fast as he could, his legs burning as he strained to breathe against his exertion.*

That said, once the manuscript reads well, it's time to consider how it will be presented for submission. On that note, it's time for two more checklists.

Format checklist:

1. If submitting on paper, use standard 8.5 x 11 inch white paper, printed on one side, with margins of one inch all around.
2. Be mindful of paragraph structure. Shifts between characters, events, and character dialog will require paragraph breaks.
3. Separate sections of narrative with a blank space, three asterisks centered, and then another blank space. While there are stylistic variations on the symbols used, remember that the symbols should not distract the reader from the narrative flow.
4. If you haven't already, at the minimum please do run a Spell/ Grammar check!

Final checklist:

1. No matter to whom your submission is heading, be sure to double check the submission guidelines and make sure you adhere to the instructions.
2. It may sound silly, but be sure your contact information is on the first page of your submission and/or cover letter.
3. Even with electronic submissions, be sure you include full contact information. This includes name, pseudonym, if used, email, mailing address, and phone number.
4. By the way, this is your very last chance to find those little gaffs by using a Spell/Grammar check.

Point of view: differentiating 1st, 2nd, and 3rd Person Narrative

THE FOUR MOST BASIC PARTS of a story are character, plot, setting, and narrative point of view. While there are many different approaches to character, plot, and setting, narrative view is the essential element used to convey the story to a reader.

Narrative perspective is often an instinctual consideration when crafting a particular story. For new authors, however, it's important to understand the characteristics of these different perspectives before writing a story. Narrative point of view has the single greatest impact on a story's telling and what literary techniques will be available to the author.

First Person

This is perhaps the most identifiable form of narrative perspective, as it incorporates the narrator directly as the storyteller.

In recent years first person narratives have proven themselves particularly popular. Any story where the character's voice is synonymous with the narrative is done in first person. Given its nature, this narrative form can be very direct, and sometimes can be a natural choice for first-time authors, as it allows the aforementioned blending of character and narrative. Grammar rules can be relaxed with a first person narrative, as the narrative voice will emulate the character's spoken voice. First person also incorporates the advantage of immediacy for a reader; nothing can entice a reader more than perusing the opening of a first person story: "I was wandering down the street one day when the most peculiar thing happened to me ..."

That said, there are inescapable aspects to a first person narrative that an author must keep in mind. To start with, remember that if the narrative and character are one and the same, the narrative cannot depict anything outside the character's physical perceptions. Depending on the plot of the story in question, this may introduce some challenges in depicting plot action outside of the character's presence. If the character isn't present, then by direct correlation the action cannot be directly present in the narrative.

To maintain realism it's also important to remember the physical limitations of human senses. A "normal" human can only see or hear so many things, particularly in tense or suspenseful situations. Characters who perceive and process minutiae during tense moments will defy believability unless they are in possession of some unusual trait.

It's also important with first person not to get lost in the character's voice. The point of a story, after all, is to propel a plot to resolution. A narrative that gets bogged down in tangential thoughts doesn't reflect a weakness of first person form but rather a flaw in the story's narrative structure. The fact that a narrative uses first person form doesn't permit an author to violate the essential elements of plot cohesion and suspense. On this same thought, great care needs to be exercised when writing a first person narrative with a dialect. There's a fine balance between loosening grammatical standards to portray an accurate dialect and losing those standards in a narrative that doesn't effectively translate to the reader's comprehension.

Another form of first person narrative is a multi-point or floating first person, where the narrative is divided into sections representing the first person narrative of each character. This can allow the author to then depict events from different characters' perspectives that a single first person narrative wouldn't permit. While this is a distinct advantage, the author must remain conscious of the fact that recounting an event from several different first person perspectives runs the risk of unnecessary repetition. Think of it as watching excessive reruns of instant replay footage. One view is good, a second view can reveal something new, a third can add another interpretation, but continuing on with additional views can deflate the tension from the moment in question.

Second Person

The hallmark of the second person narrative is for an author to directly address readers, thereby casting them as participants within the narrative. Second person narrative is cued by the use of "you", "your", and "yours."

For the most part, this form of narrative expression is seen in non-fiction, though it makes rare appearances in fiction. In fact, in this primer I often switch to second person narrative when discussing subjective issues that you—there it is!—as an individual author might have to consider. On the other hand, for other parts I switch to third person, using the generic pronouns "author" or "authors" to discuss issues that are more objective in nature. Likewise, when citing my personal experiences in parts of this primer I also switch to first person—as I just did.

I'm citing this primer as an example to contrast the use of second person narrative in fiction. The book you hold in your hands is a work of non-fiction; it's essentially an instructional guide. In technical or instructional writing the author is allowed some leeway to alternate between first, second, and third person address to effectively discuss the included topics.

That said, the rules for nonfiction and fiction are quite different. Whereas nonfiction makes allowances for narrative switches, this is a decided no-no in fiction. In fact, authors who commit the error of narrative switches in fiction are often dismissed as inexperienced. To those who are new to writing it often seems a nitpicking technicality until they understand the negative impact such switches have on narrative flow.

While there are instances in first person narratives such as a character *discussing* rather than *narrating* a point in the story—a first to second person perspective switch—it's safe to say there are no allowances in third person for such transgressions. The reason for this is a narrative fundamental: the job of an author is to *show* a story, not *tell* a story. Once a narrative makes a second person switch, it moves headlong toward telling rather showing.

So what's the reality of writing in the second person? Simply put, it's a rare case indeed where the second person perspective is used in fiction with success. Too often it serves as little more than an open door to the pitfalls of narrative switches. Instead, choose either first or third person perspective, settle into your narrative, and then *show* readers your story.

Third Person

Last but not least, third person narrative allows the author two specific options: *omniscient third person* and *limited third person*.

As the label *omniscient* suggests, in the omniscient form the author is allowed to be all-knowing and all-seeing within the narrative. In this form, consider the author's perspective as a floating viewpoint, with the ability to move from character to character in each section. This is similar to a floating first person narrative, with the difference being that the narrative voice stands apart from the character. This form also allows the author to narrate on a grand scale, meaning that the narration can evolve independent of any character to stand on its own feet. The inverse is also allowable, wherein a narration can flow independent of any character and then focus on a particular individual. Such a shift will be displayed in the narrative example below.

As opposed to omniscient third person, in limited third person the author presents the entire narrative from one character's view. In this form, imagine the author's perspective as a balloon floating behind the character. This narrative allows the author to portray all of the character's thoughts and emotions while retaining an independent narrative voice. The key difference between this form and the omniscient form is that the narrative will be limited—hence the label—to what the subject character experiences or understands, similar to the limitation of a first person narrative.

Perhaps the biggest challenge to using either of the third person narrative forms is the burden it places upon the author. Whereas first person narratives challenge an author to create a character compelling enough to sustain the weight of a story, third person allows the author to engage the reader with a single character—limited third—or multiple characters—omniscient third—*in addition* to an independent narrative voice. In effect the author becomes a bard of many hats. A multi-point first person narrative will comprise the same challenge.

✦

REGARDLESS OF THE NARRATIVE FORM employed in a story, it's imperative for the author to understand at all times the limits of narrative judgment. Readers embrace stories where judgments and opinions of character and plot action derive from the characters themselves, not from the narrative. In first person this issue is abated by the fact that narrative and character voices are one in the same. In third person narrative form, however, the narration is a separate voice. A common pitfall for developing authors is to inject their opinions and judgments into the narrative. In these narrative forms the narrator is impartial and without opinion; only characters should express opinions. It's up to the author to provide the descriptive framework of what a character might experience, but actual *impressions* and *emotional responses* must be couched in the character's perspective.

This can be a fine line at times. Remember a simple standard. If an opinion or judgment is framed in the context of a character, it's allowable. If the opinion or judgment stands outside any character reference, then it's a narrative interjection and isn't allowed. In either third person form, the narrative voice is always neutral. Once again, it's perfectly acceptable to describe the *objective* aspects of a situation as the narrator, but any *subjective* reactions or interpretations must be presented through the characters. Descriptive neutrality can be a subtle yet very powerful tool in both first and third person narratives, as it allows readers a hidden bystander's perspective on a character's actions and responses.

Let's take a look at a sample passage presented in first person, first person with second person switching, third person limited, and third person omniscient form.

First person:

I was walking down the street on a sunny afternoon when the comet struck downtown. I remember the white flash in my sight and the mule-like kick of the shockwave in my chest before I was blown off my feet. At least I guess I was blown off my feet. It was the only reasonable way to explain what happened when I came to my senses, because I was back at the end of my driveway where I had started my walk.

My ears buzzed from the roar of the impact. Later I would think that was a good thing. Being deaf for a few minutes let me escape the screams of the wounded.

First person, with second person switching (note the use of 'you'):

I was walking down the street on a sunny afternoon when the comet struck downtown. I remember the white flash in my sight and the mule-like kick of the shockwave in my chest before I was blown off my feet. At least I guess I was blown off my feet. It was the only reasonable way to explain what happened when I came to my senses, because I was back at the end of my driveway where I had started my walk.

My ears buzzed from the roar of the impact. It took a moment or two for me to get my head straight and start absorbing what was around me—and what was around me was like nothing I'd seen before.

There's a common wisdom that says you don't know who you really are until your back is to the wall. Let me tell you, standing there in a world turned upside down, I wasn't sure who I was going to be. No matter how many times you see disasters on the news nothing can prepare you for the way it plays out when you're standing in one. What you see is one thing, but what you smell is another. It takes a day or two. Rotting leaves, rotting sewage, rotting garbage, and then the worst of it—rotting bodies.

But that was yet to come. In those first moments, all I had was the buzz in my ears. Later I would think that was a good thing. Being deaf for a few minutes let me escape the screams of the wounded.

Third person limited:

John was walking down the street on a sunny afternoon when the comet struck downtown. His sight flashed white before the shockwave hit his chest with the ferocity of a mule's kick to blast him off his feet. He flew through the air until gravity dragged him down to the rumbling ground, the only saving grace of his impact the loose soil in the garden bed at the end of his driveway. So he lay, sprawled and deafened by the blast, until he shook off his daze and looked around.

The quiet suburban street he once knew was gone, replaced by an apocalyptic nightmare of shattered homes and shredded trees. Deafened by the blast, he looked through his delirium to the odd distensions of his neighbors' faces as their screams washed unheard past his ears.

Third person omniscient (note the shift to third person limited from first to second paragraph):

The comet's trajectory had been decided long before man ever walked on two feet, dictated by the intricate interplay of gravity and celestial mechanics. Indeed it may have passed over the blue sky that enclosed John's comfortable little world several times over the millennia. Unseen, it nevertheless moved closer to its date of doom with each eccentric orbital cycle until the fateful day when hammer met anvil. What John didn't know as he walked down the street from his driveway was that he had a front row seat for a cataclysm defying the limits of comprehension afforded by his serene existence.

The blast sent out a flash of white light in the superheated moment of impact, followed by an imperceptible delay before the shockwave of compressed air bowled John from his feet. Houses were shattered, trees were shorn of their leaves, and his neighbors were torn from the carefree bliss of their lives to find themselves as nothing more than extra debris among the devastation. Their screams rose as their minds perceived the horror enveloping them, their anguish washing unheard over John's prone form.

He shook off his daze as he propped himself up on his elbows and blinked in bewilderment at the new reality thrust upon him. It took a moment to realize he was mired in the loose garden soil at the end of his driveway.

✹

IN THESE HEAVY-HANDED EXAMPLES, THE differences in narrative expression should be apparent. The descriptive elements in the first person narrative are limited to John's direct sensory input, whereas the third person limited allows some deeper description. The third person omniscient allows the greatest description beyond John's character; indeed, in this example, the comet is almost characterized as much as John. Nevertheless, the comet is irrelevant without its effect on John. Likewise, the only reason for the first person and third person limited narratives to exist is their linkage to John.

On the other hand, the use of first person with a second person switch attempts to drag the reader directly into the story environment. What's important to note in the second person switch is that the same effect could be generated elsewhere in this hypothetical passage with first person description, rather than jarring the narrative flow for a direct reader address.

In regard to John's environment, again we can see how the first person—and to a lesser degree the third person limited—narrative form constrains the descriptive elements external to John. Due to the narrative linkage to John in first person and third person limited, we as the readers don't get to see the greater story of the comet's impact. Not so with the third person omniscient, where we witness the entire event from impending doom to the immediate moments thereafter.

These examples need to be framed with my personal disclaimer that, as an author, I'm most comfortable writing in third person limited and omniscient. I mention this to illustrate the final point that every author has to find a narrative form in which he or she feels most comfortable. There are some authors who only write in first person, while there are others who dabble, depending on the story. No matter what narrative perspective one chooses for a particular story, it's important to remember that the perspective chosen will have an indelible impact on not only the writing of the story but the ultimate expression of the completed piece.

That said, and aside from all heated debates on the merits of one form of narrative perspective over another, the simple truth is that any narrative form will fail without a compelling character and plot. At the end of the day, it's the author's responsibility to make stories that live beyond the page through character and plot development. Regardless of narrative perspective, characters that fail to engage a reader will sabotage a story. Characters are the reader's portals into a story. If characters are not emotionally involved in the story, then there's no reason for a reader to be involved.

Well, that sounds like the perfect segue for our next section, the importance of character development.

Characterization: summoning life within a story

NARRATIVES OF ANY LENGTH CAN live or die on the success of their character depiction. Whether a story is one thousand words or one hundred thousand words in length, the humanity of the characters serves as the reader's sole link to the story in question.

One of the fascinating aspects of writing a story and summoning characters is that it gives an author the opportunity to delve the mind of an entirely different personality. A successful character is more than a physical description or collection of trademark phrases and gestures. Such descriptions are encompassed by the terms *characterization* and *characteristics*, which are not to be confused with *character*. A successful character transcends the page through cohesive depiction of thought, action, and emotion.

It may sound obvious, but characters need to be human. They must embody the same range of complexities that an actual person can possess, regardless of the objective "health" of the character's psyche. This doesn't mean that an author has to be a psychologist to construct a fictional psyche; nevertheless, writing requires authors to be students of the human condition. After developing a few characters, it's not uncommon for an author to feel like an armchair psychologist. By nature, writing requires a great deal of introspection. This one quality is perhaps the most human characteristic that sets us apart as individuals. Likewise it should be so for characters.

Metaphysical mumbo-jumbo? Quite the opposite. A story without compelling characters is a set of circumstances. A weak story with good characters can stand on its own, whereas a good story with weak characters will most likely fail to hold anyone's interest.

Developing a character can seem like a monumental task, bearing some similarities to developing a plot. In both cases the author must go in stages, being careful not to divulge too much while not keeping too much under wraps. For readers, the characters who have become near and dear to the author during the writing process are first met as strangers. Readers find their way into a character in the same manner that they find their way into a plot. The best example for this is the success of characters in novel series. If the character strikes a cord with readers, those readers are likely to come back for more.

When writing, it's important to treat your characters like real people. Behavioral aspects of living people are readily portable to fictional characters, as well they should. People learn and grow through life events. People change through things they experience and individuals they meet. All people, on some level, are guided by hindsight interpretations of their life. These engines of change combine to produce the process known as *catharsis*. On a similar note, people employ introspection on various levels to guide their decisions. Characters should possess all these ingredients. How many an author can explore, and how deep the exploration can go, will depend on the length and complexity of the story the characters inhabit.

So what makes a character seem real within a story? First and foremost a character must be invested in the narrative. As I said in the last section, characters serve as the reader's portals into a story. During the progression of a story, a character must be challenged and changed in some way by the plot events; once again, it's this process of catharsis that forms one of the primary elements of a successful story.

Catharsis serves a two-fold purpose: one, it maintains cohesion by making the character integral to the story; two, it conveys meaning to the story by the change it evokes within the character. Depending on the nature of a given story, the change can be a positive or negative direction. When "positive" and "negative" become subjective gray zones rather than moralistic absolutes, an author has truly hit the humanistic mark for a character.

The cathartic process doesn't require a character to be an amorphous pile of goo waiting to be shaped as the story dictates. The truth is quite the contrary. The character should have just as much influence on the plot events as the plot events have on the character. This is necessary in order to reflect part one of the two-fold purpose mentioned above, the cohesion of character and story. If the character is successfully invested in the story, the character will own that story. This allows the character's decisions to have direct influence on future plot events even as past plot events influence the character.

Consider character depiction to be built in layers. The lowest layer consists of the immutable personality traits you choose for your character. These things won't change in presence, but can change in expression, given a potent plot event. Catharsis occurs at this level. For example a character may by loyal only to have the focus of that loyalty shift as the story develops. The next layer can be composed of beliefs and impressions the character has learned through the life he or she inhabits at the beginning of the story. These can be used during the plot as inroads for catharsis and openings for introspection. The outer layer is how the character physically inhabits the story. This covers a range of possibilities, including expressions, particular dialog phrases, choice in dress, possession of a treasured item—the list is potentially endless.

With this rough construct in mind, the author can then consider how these layers will be explored and revealed over the course of the story. Typically, this begins from the outside and works its way in, much the way we get to know people in real life. Narrative creativity allows for other options. A story may open with a dramatic event that speaks volumes about a character before a single mention of physical appearance.

Remember that the believability of a story depends on character. Readers are very sensitive to drastic, unexplained changes in characters because it's a natural warning sign when interacting with real people. Just as with real people, characters won't transform their personality without some cause.

Writing dialog: giving characters their voice

ONE OF THE FUNDAMENTAL ASPECTS of building characters is crafting their dialog. For some authors this comes quite naturally, while for others dialog can be one of the most challenging aspects of writing. Either way there are several crucial facets of dialog to understand. The best advice for writing dialog is to understand that, as an author, you now have the ability to use your author's ear to listen to the ways real people speak. It can be the best reference guide for crafting dialog within a written work.

To state the obvious, dialog is the written expression of an oral exchange between characters. As such it consists of the spoken word. The reality of speech between people is that grammar most often goes out the window. The neurological process of speech is incredibly complex and dynamic. While people speak, ideas can often shift and evolve in ways that may make perfect sense to a listener but sound ridiculous to a reader.

The first rule of dialog is to understand that although grammar rules can be greatly relaxed to reflect the genuine ways in which people talk, the dialog must still make sense to the reader. In the section regarding narrative points of view, I mentioned that even when working with dialect, the author must take great care to ensure the narrative context can still transfer to the reader. This holds true for dialog as well. If the goal is to portray a passage of dialog that is indecipherable to a character, it's often in the best interest of the author to reflect this through narrative description rather than in actual written dialog.

The second rule of dialog is to keep it relevant to the momentum of the narrative. Readers don't need to see every little verbal exchange between characters. Just as a narrative can be overburdened with descriptive elements that detract from the progression of a story, so too extraneous dialog can overburden the progression of a story. Dialog is no different than any other aspect of a story. If it doesn't serve a particular purpose in the overall maturation of the story, then most likely it doesn't need to be included.

The third rule of dialog is how it relates to the structure of a given character. Different people express themselves in different ways; indeed, it can be said that how individuals speak is one of the hallmarks of personality. This holds true as well for fictional characters, and it most often manifests as a matter of consistency. People of certain backgrounds, encompassing everything from socio-economics, education, and ethnicity to geographical influence, religion, and philosophy, will have certain associated predilections in their manner of speech. This isn't to say one determines the other; that's an exercise that can rapidly degenerate to cliché stereotypes.

The point is to a deeper consideration: as authors we create a canvas of properties to build the personality of a character, and all those properties combine to produce the way in which that character speaks. If great effort is taken to portray a character a certain way, yet the character speaks in a very different way, there has to be some explanation for this in the narrative. For example if a character is a college professor, but routinely spouts gutter profanity, there has to be some accounting for this within the story. Once again don't forget that readers have an innate sensitivity for inconsistencies of character. The last thing you want as an author is for readers to stop cold and shake their heads in confusion.

A fourth rule for writing dialog is to understand that a spoken exchange between characters is a little story within the overall story. Verbal exchanges between real people follow this same basic rule. I specifically use the phrase *verbal exchange* to illustrate the point that dialog is an *interaction* between people. Those interactions may not always be apparent to outsiders, but for at least one of the people or characters involved in the exchange, it stems from a specific motivation and serves a particular purpose. These need not be momentous items. In terms of narrative and character development, a stream of dialog in which characters seem only to be killing time can be used to develop deep yet subtle inroads to the core of one or more participants.

The fifth rule of dialog is not to be heavy-handed or overly dramatic. As living people we all know the gut reaction to people who make grandiose statements, and it usually comes as a shake of the head or roll of the eyes in dismissal. If a particular character is given to dramatic indulgences, then such statements are merely a reflection of that character's personality. Other than that, dramatic statements from characters have to be used with care.

This leads to perhaps the final concern for dialog, and that is whether or not it sounds natural. The best guide to determine this is also the simplest of exercises, and that is to read your dialog aloud. If it sounds the way actual people might talk, then you know you're on target. If it sounds cumbersome, too mechanistic, or if you trip over the phrase structure of the dialog itself, it's best to consider revision.

If all this sounds more like something actors might do, then congratulations are in order. You've just realized that part of bringing characters to life is to summon them as their own living beings, which is a fundamental part of the acting process.

It's a great moment when characters transition from mere concepts to whole entities that can walk and talk within a story. Once you reach that moment, it's time to put them to work—and that, of course, is the job of a story's plot. Segue!

Plotting: getting from beginning to end

IT SEEMS LIKE A SIMPLE idea that a plot guides readers from the first word to the last. Plot may seem the most obvious mechanical part of a story of any length, yet a story's plot has to function on more levels than a reader might recognize. On the other hand, the author must keep those levels in mind at all times. Good technique will keep readers engaged with characters, while bad technique can be evidenced through a range of negative reader impressions.

The most common plotting errors include a story that took too long to develop, ended abruptly, committed the sin of plot conceit by omitting an essential element until the very end, lacked sufficient impetus for character motivation, failed to properly evolve from one event to the next, or closed with unresolved character interactions, unresolved subplots, unexplained plot events, and/or extraneous plot events.

When considering plotting, the word *immediacy* is often used as a measuring stick of good technique. Common wisdom dictates that a story should start as close as possible to its principal or motivating event. Underlying story elements can be woven in through flashback, hindsight, or subplots. Be cautious, however, that this wisdom isn't misconstrued to mean that the main event of a plot has to happen right away. A principal plot event is one that serves as the story's motivation. It not only gives the story reason, it propels it forward. The main event will then be the culmination of the story.

Consider one of the most common plot conventions, the revenge story. The motivating event is often the loss of a loved one, while the culminating event is the actual act of revenge. Another common construct is the murder story. The murder is the motivating event; solving its mystery and catching the killer comprise the culminating events.

Plot will of course have a major influence on the length of a story and the intricacy of its characters. If the intention of a story is to evoke a major change in a character, the plot may require more time to develop along with the character to successfully elicit the gravity of an event that evokes said change. On the other hand a story that is itself influenced by a character's composition may be shorter in length.

There are more variables in this equation than several volumes of discussion could ever cover, but two examples may serve well to illustrate the point. Tolstoy's *Anna Karenina* appears to have a rather simple story on the surface: wife meets man, they have an affair, and social mess ensues. Simple, right? Wrong. Beneath this simple arc is an expansive set of subplots and character interactions working together to bring to life the society Tolstoy depicts. It's a massive book because it's a sweeping portrayal of every aspect of the reality his characters inhabit. Without this depth of development, the social travails of its characters would lack dramatic impact.

A second example, and opposed in length to Tolstoy's *Anna Karenina*, is Kafka's *The Metamorphosis*. Essentially a novella, it takes a reader on the surreal exploration of a man who wakes one day to find himself transformed to a giant insect. It's a reality-defying event that translates to the reader through the depiction and interaction of a handful of characters. The immediacy of the story complements its claustrophobic nature.

With those philosophical considerations aside, the nuts-and-bolts process of narrative progression remains. This entails how the written structure of the narrative conveys the story to the reader. Remember that plot and characters exist in an action-reaction couplet so that the action of one will influence the other. An event happened, so characters had to respond. A character made a choice, so an event was set in motion or influenced. As the plot builds, the story should challenge the characters to keep them emotionally invested within the narrative. Once an event sets off an emotional process within a character, that character's behavior within succeeding plot events is correspondingly shaped by that process. A sure plotting miscue for a reader is when a character's emotions flip on and off without explanation.

Explanation is an important issue. In terms of narrative semantics, explanation can be considered an improper term, because good story telling will *show* why things are happening through character inter-action, plot events, narrative description, or a combination of these elements. It is with rare success that a story can stop and allow an author space to give readers a lesson in some plot point. In the vast majority of cases, this is considered an error because it stops the story dead in its tracks.

Good story technique will provide plot opportunities that show how things within a story tie together. A handy piece of advice is that something nonessential to the development of the story has no place in the story. Longer narratives allow space for little interludes that may not seem essential to the plot but serve a secondary cause to develop character. Readers should never end up with the impression that they burrowed through a section of narrative with no clear purpose or function within the overall story. One of the things an author doesn't want to hear is that a reader started "skimming for something to happen."

The natural progression of these considerations is plot momentum. This shouldn't be confused as a belief that something has to be "happen-ing" in every paragraph of a story. It all depends on the type of story. Even a plot that embodies a great deal of physical action will lose momentum if there's no clear cause of events or progression of an overriding story. At the other end of the spectrum resides what can be thought of as slow-burn stories where the plot builds toward a moment of impact. While these stories may seem to lack outward action, the plot gains momentum by the author building suspense through character development and suggestive sub-plotting. Gothic tales are excellent examples.

Although there's a macroscopic view of plot momentum that applies to an entire narrative, there's also a microscopic view that focuses momentum through scene transitions. Whether it's a movement between scenes within a chapter or a movement from chapter to chapter, narrative transitions should flow into each other. Consider each section of a narrative as its own little story that also has to leave an opening for the next section of narrative. This is an excellent way to keep a reader hungry for more and often leads people to describe a story as a *page-turner*. Book-length stories can comprise several plot arcs, such that some close in pivotal scenes, while the overriding plot arc continues to propel the book forward.

Nevertheless, it takes practice to develop good plot momentum. The linkage between successive scenes serves as the foundation to spur reader curiosity—and thereby, reader interest—as to what will happen next. For example in a few sections of this primer I've made blatant indications of segue opportunities to succeeding sections. While there was an intent to introduce a bit of levity, I made those indications to illustrate the point of flow. In any given story there may be several different orders in which to stage the individual scenes of a narrative, but it's the author's responsibility to find the optimal balance between plot cohesion, narrative sensibility, and reader interest.

When it's time to sit down and plot a story, there are two approaches. Some authors prefer a thorough and strict outline. Once the outline is done, they flesh out the narrative to bring the story to life. The other approach is less formal but somewhat more organic; rather than an outline, there's only a basic understanding of where the story should end, with concepts for a few key moments progressing toward that end.

Choosing one over the other is certainly a matter of comfort rather than of right versus wrong. Naturally, longer stories will necessitate some type of loose outline to maintain plot cohesion. For stories that are driven more by character, a less rigid outline can allow space for character development. Stories that are written from a strict outline have a methodical advantage, yet care must be taken to ensure the reader doesn't have the impression that the plot is satisfying a checklist rather than following a natural progression.

As a final note on plots, be careful when employing random events in a plot. In some cases the presence of random events can be used as a plot device to make a point within the story, but this can be a precarious approach. Readers are naturally attuned to a logical progression of events because evolution has built an innate desire for order in the human mind's capacity to organize abstract thought—and make no mistake that a work of fiction is an exercise of a reader's abstract thought process.

Neuroscience aside, if a plot hits readers with random events too often, readers will become frustrated. Readers want to follow a plot. They want structure. They *don't* want to be manipulated. When a story turns at the last moment on one point that has been completely hidden from the reader, it's considered a story *conceit*. In effect it's as if the author cheated. A plot revelation or twist is something that will be seen as intrinsic to the overall structure of the story upon its reveal, whereas a plot conceit exists completely outside of the narrative scope until it crashes into the narrative.

The best example of this is the plot device where the story events are revealed to be a dream. This type of story device is a *revelation* when there are subtle clues throughout the story that something may not be quite right. When the revelation occurs, the narrative should recall those clues and knit them together to reveal how the story exists cohesively within the plot device. On the other hand, the dream device is a plot *conceit* when there is no clue; the story chugs along and suddenly ends with the character waking up. To readers this conveys a dismal message: I, the author, was too lazy to figure out how to end my story, so oh-well it's all a dream and the character wakes up—zing!—the end. If you were to read such a story, you wouldn't be satisfied either.

With these overall considerations in mind, it's time to take a simplified look at some time-proven plot techniques. The following labels are subjective, that is, it's the way I label them, rather than formal classifications.

- *Linear plot:* The story flows in one ordered time sequence, like letters in an alphabet.
- *Nonlinear plot:* The story has an overall progression, but individual scenes follow a subjective, contextual order rather than a temporal order; think stories that rely on flashbacks.
- *Top-down approach:* A central character possessing full knowledge of underlying situations contacts another character that must be taught the situations.
- *Bottom-up approach:* A central character is brought into an unknown situation and encounters other characters that have full knowledge of the situation.
- *Outside-in approach:* A character attempts to change an established order from the outside; typically, the established order is not benevolent. Think stories of investigators or revolution material.
- *Inside-out approach:* A character attempts to change an established order from the inside; the established order will either be revealed as antagonistic or the character's actions taken in the goal of correcting some errant deviation of the established order. Think whistle-blower stories.

These techniques aren't rigid and can be blended to take on different forms. Combining them with variations of narrative perspective only adds to the mix. As a simple example from cinema, *The Matrix* is a linear, bottom-up, outside-in approach presented in third person perspective. Aside from a few scenes, it's all from Neo's view.

A story is a recipe of elements consisting of characters, narrative perspective, and plotting. The only question left to address is setting. Sounds like an opportune moment for the next segue …

Setting: story environment and world building

When sitting down to write a story, the elements of character, narrative perspective, and plotting are intrinsic realities that receive consideration by default. Setting, however, is somewhat different. While the story must take place in some physical space, an author has some leeway in dealing with this particular element. Depending on the story, setting can be everything or it can be somewhat irrelevant, other than delineating character and event locations.

Story environment

From a narrative standpoint, setting is much more than the notion of where a story takes place. It also includes a notion of time, not just in terms of a season but also past, contemporary, or future dates. From these basic considerations stem the concept that *setting* is really something more complex, something that can be thought of as *story environment*. This stretches the definition and concept of setting. In this expanded scope it includes the idea of how the environment in which the characters exist impacts them and perhaps the plot as well.

In terms of creating a cohesive reality within the narrative of a story, looking at setting in the bigger perspective of a story environment allows you to weave new elements into the story. Literary tradition certainly poses an argument for story environment being one of the most often used elements for symbolic or metaphorical subtexts.

That said, the greater a role story environment plays within the narrative, the more attention the author must pay to the detail of the environment. If there's a particular point to a story that it's cold outside, then there should be subtle tweaks to the narrative to show how the cold impacts the characters. People dress and behave differently in the cold. Weather can have an impact on the ways in which people meet and socialize. It changes the types of foods people choose to eat and how they respond to said foods.

Once again there's a requirement for the author to be a studious observer of the human condition to bring humanity to the narrative. More to the point, characters who deviate from the expected norm of a setting can offer fertile ground for dialog, interaction, and development.

There's a saying that authors should write what they know. When it comes to story environment, it's important for authors to take note of the background knowledge they might hold. It's human nature that what we experience as commonplace often fades from our direct perception. As an author, some thought can summon those experiences to the forefront of the creative mind for translation into a story as valuable descriptive resources.

To continue with the example above, writing that it's cold isn't enough. Think about what it means to be cold from personal experience and relate it through the characters. This is a powerful tool when writing a story with a very specific setting or environment with which the author is familiar but which can be new to readers. The author can lend veracity through description, while also knowing how much the environment can be manipulated for the sake of the story.

World building

The extreme of story environment is the process of *world building*. To a certain extent a case can be made that every story has a bit of world building due to the returning concern that characters require a physical space in which to interact.

For the most part contemporary stories don't employ world building unless the author is making a specific point of describing a fictional place in present time. World building is a specialty of genre fiction such as historical fiction, fantasy fiction, speculative fiction, and science fiction. Contemporary supernatural or horror fiction might employ world building to describe a fictional reality hidden from our common, shared reality.

How do you go about building a fictional world? History is a great guide because it teaches us generalized lessons about societies. It's human nature to build social orders, no matter how chaotic or anarchic that society may appear from the outside. Indeed, it's the process of social ordering that allows civilizations to exist. The correlation to fiction is that any kind of fictional world must operate on some context of rules. This structure allows the world to function and also provides a glimpse of the forces motivating its existence. History again is a great guide because it also teaches us that every known society has in part shaped its social order as a response to interaction with the surrounding world. A societal order must provide some means to support the survival of the social group. When this linkage fails, the society itself will fail.

Careful consideration must be taken as to how a society functions in the fictional world in relation to how it shapes the mindset of the characters living within its social order. A common error with world building is to describe a certain kind of society and then focus on a character that isn't just at odds with that order, but who thinks and talks like someone from our common society. There will always be dissidents, trendsetters, and trailblazers to pioneer a new path within a society, but they will embark on that path in the context of the society they know. Their objections will be in response to whatever component of the societal order they reject. The way they phrase their objections will be couched in the way they've been educated or trained to think, and even their actions may be heavily influenced by what they know of their world. Introducing an outsider or transplanting the character to a different societal order to influence the character's thought offers plot possibilities to loosen some of those constraints.

Remember as well, when considering a fictional world, that some aspects can be taken at face value and won't require explanation, unless explanation is required by the story or plot. This dilemma is often encountered in science fiction where futuristic devices that defy our current technological capacity are often employed. The criticism sometimes heard is that an author failed to describe how these devices might work. This is unfounded because there may be no need for the author to describe how these devices work.

The example I often make for this involves two characters taking a ride on the subway. While they're on the subway having a conversation, there's absolutely no need to describe the working of the subway. All the reader needs to know is that the subway leaves from point A and gets the characters to point B. How the subway works, the mechanical properties of its motors and brakes, the electric demands of a third rail, and the materials of the subway car are all irrelevant—unless, that is, the characters are having a conversation about something pertinent to one of those systems. In that case it's incumbent upon the author to not only have a plan as to how something works, but more importantly, how it might be made *not* to work.

Remember that just about everything that exists within a society exists for some reason, even if that reason is impossibly convoluted. A quick view of our society is a good example because it's full of processes that may seem beyond explanation on their surface. Some research will often reveal a set of circumstances and reasons that allowed the thing or process to exist. For the most part, though, human society is quite effective at jettisoning things that serve no purpose. *Tradition* is the compulsion to hold such things in place, while *innovation* is the process that seeks to turn them aside, and the conflict between these two has fueled many dramas, both real and fictional. Just as these processes exist in our common world, they should exist within a fictional world as well. A static society doesn't have a promising future, and the appearance of a static society often hides forces of change until they explode. The old Soviet system's calamitous failure is a perfect example.

There's hardly a societal system that hasn't been tried at least once in the recorded follies of humanity. For authors interested in world building, history can provide real examples of different societies. In addition history can provide the background knowledge of how those societies rose and, perhaps of greater importance, how they fell.

Narrative perspective, characters, plot and setting—once everything is set and the story is written, that's that, right? Guess again. Time for a little something known as editing.

Levels of editing: copy, line, and content edit

IN THE SECTION ON BASIC writing mechanics, I stressed the importance of editing your work, with the barest minimum consisting of a spell/grammar check within a word processor. The reality is that you must consider a greater investment in editorial attention if you truly want to see your writing succeed.

A common error among inexperienced authors is to think that editing does indeed consist of little more than clicking on their word processor's Spell/Grammar check button. For those who don't even use this most basic level of editing, they should strongly consider it if they are indeed ready to send out their work. Although proofreading and revision are editorial exercises, their rudimentary natures are almost synonymous with the actual writing of a particular story. A common practice of authors who've gained some experience, myself included, is to go through numerous proofs of their work before considering it ready for a serious editorial eye.

The editing levels discussed below are more formal exercises to bring a piece of writing up to market expectation. Editing comes in three levels, and each level embodies a different perspective.

Copy edit

Copy edit can be thought of as the lowest form of editing. It involves the mechanics within your individual sentences, focusing on proper word usage, grammar rules, and spelling. At this level there's less focus on sentence flow or the overall delivery of the story at hand. A transcript without a proper copy edit will not work because flaws at this level jar a reader from the story by stumbling over words.

Nevertheless, some people still confuse this basic level of editing with the function built into their word processor's Spell/Grammar check. While software is a good, solid start to this edit, software cannot properly interpret all the subtleties of narrative language. Software checks operate on formal grammar rules; literary language can bend those rules.

One must be particularly cautious with this stage of editing when employing a dialect.

Line edit

This is the second level of editing and involves how the individual sentences flow into paragraphs. The focus here, particularly for those new to writing, will concern whether the narrative *shows* a story rather than *tells* a story. For those unfamiliar with the difference in these terms, perhaps a simple analogy will prove best. When the narrative tells a story, it reads more like a lab report, whereas a narrative that shows a story will grow from the page into its own reality within the reader's mind.

Content edit

This last level of editing takes a macroscopic view to judge the overall development of the story. At this level, judgments are made regarding the revision of entire sections of narrative, the addition or deletion of characters and/or scenes, alterations in plot or mending inconsistencies in plot arcs, and the sensitive issue of manuscript length. Content edit may have the shortest description, but it can be the most difficult level of editing. Changes from the content perspective can require authors to take a truly objective look at their work, which will require them to abandon misplaced sentiment for elements that detract from a story's success.

Objectivity is a crucial issue in the realm of content editing. In the realms of copy and line editing, the editorial evaluation and requirements are often straightforward because they involve basic mechanics of good grammar and prose. Changes—or perhaps *improvements* is a better word—at these levels often impart an immediate sense toward the maturation of the written work as a piece of professional fiction. Content editing, on the other hand, requires an author to look at something that may be mechanically functional yet manifests as a narrative flaw within the greater story context.

Only an objective examination will allow an author to spot these flaws. Subjectively, the author's opinion can be clouded by the emotional investment in some of these flawed sections such that the author can fail to see their extraneous nature. For this reason the content edit should be handled by an outside editor. In the realm of short stories, a content edit is within an author's capacity, but for book length stories it's all too common—and all too easy—for an author to get mystified by the complexity of his or her creation and lose objectivity.

❋

When looking at a completed manuscript, these three levels of editing can often mingle, particularly the process of line and copy edits. In some cases larger plot issues that fall into the realm of a content edit won't become apparent until clearing the clutter of line and copy edits. Consider editing as similar to sanding a piece of wood. Each pass of the sander brings you closer to the true surface of the wood as it simultaneously reveals less and less noticeable imperfections.

Editing is a slow and patient process, and there's no practical way to rush and have it meet with any success. In short, a quick edit is a sloppy edit. Editing is, however, a process just as vital to a manuscript as the actual writing itself. Without a thorough edit you shouldn't even consider a piece for submission. Editors, agents, and publishers have a keen eye to spot unrefined manuscripts. If an author fails to take these editorial steps, it's a blatant sign that the author isn't quite serious or professional in his or her efforts. Remember that while writing may be a dreamy hobby for you, it's a profession for people in the publication business. Proper editorial efforts constitute one of the best ways to signal publication professionals that you not only respect them but also the craft of your writing.

Keep in mind that any editorial steps you take on your own are sure to be repeated by professional editors during the production process of a book publication and perhaps even in the publication path of a short story market.

When enough is enough: working with explicit content

EVERY AUTHOR WILL HAVE TO gauge his or her comfort level with explicit material, no matter the intended audience. What can be considered explicit or gratuitous are matters of judgment, market sensitivity, and current literary tastes.

In recent years the border of what could be considered explicit has undergone a rather dramatic shift. Readers have not only responded with the influence of their purchase dollars but also with a general acceptance of more pointed material. How much this has to do with systemic changes in modern mass media content is a chicken-and-egg sociological discussion that transcends the realms of this primer; nevertheless, authors need to understand where their subject matter lands in the marketplace.

Consideration of explicit material falls into two principal areas. First, from the level of content editing, it's a question as to the necessity of the content—think of this as *gratuitous material*—and second, it's how the content stands in relation to the tolerance of the intended audience—a more precise context of *explicit material*. Last but not least are the concerns for explicit language in dialog and character narrative.

Gratuitous material

As discussed in the previous section on content editing, explicit material—for the moment, let's call it "highly descriptive" material—has to serve a place within the overall narrative to have its proper impact. Authors who wish to include highly descriptive material need to question themselves as to what they want to impress on their readers. Specifically, does the author want a story that seems to be an excuse to string together excessive scenes, or does an excessive scene build out of a story's natural momentum?

The answer to this question will divide reader impressions into two distinct groups. A story that serves little more purpose than to connect highly descriptive scenes runs the risk of simply seeming excessive. As with any other jarring experience, this type of presentation will either turn readers off entirely or leave them jaded. At that point the only lingering suspense will be to see what new way the author can find to shock a reading audience. The most likely result will be for readers to skim the interim narrative in search of the next "wild" scene. That's not literature, that's shock treatment. There's a rather uncomplimentary word to describe this kind of story presentation, and that word is *schlock*.

On the other hand, genuine suspense is a far more satisfying accomplishment for both reader and author. If a narrative has properly entwined its characters—and by extension its readers—then a jarring scene won't require exhaustive degrees of highly descriptive content. It's the author's responsibility to engage the reader's imagination to illustrate the scene so that the reader can absorb its detail and inhabit the scene, rather than bludgeoning the reader's imagination with an absolute rendition. In fact the old wisdom of less is more applies in all its wondrous ways.

The best way an author can judge the efficacy of such scenes is through reader reaction. If readers are *emotionally* consumed by a particular scene, they will often discuss it far out of subjective relation to the rest of the narrative, just as with any other momentous scene. I've written a number of stories with intense scenes, and I know I've hit the mark when I have to remind readers that those scenes consist of only a few paragraphs in relation to the body of the story.

Again, the best route from a literary standpoint is to show only the things that are required by the narrative. If the utmost detail is required for a particular scene to further the story, then perhaps it's justified. Just remember that scenes are in service to a story and not the reverse. Once a story is in service to its scenes, it's a sure bet the border of gratuity has been crossed.

Explicit material

While gratuitous material is something that can be judged from a structural or literary judgment of a narrative, explicit material is a much more subjective issue.

In most cases this consideration will regard how appropriate the material is for its intended audience. This isn't just a matter of age-appropriate material; those decisions are much more straightforward. Although, in today's world, it can be very difficult to judge what's considered "appropriate" for younger audiences—particularly the young adult audience. To the point, there are boundaries of acceptability within some genres. For example, fans of cozy mysteries won't be interested in a graphic tryst between two characters. Likewise, fans of Gothic horror will find graphic torture-horror out of bounds because it violates the imaginative haunting of the Gothic tradition.

On occasion authors are asked by various elements within the publishing world to provide a rating for their material, such as PG, PG-13, R, or "adult content." While such ratings delineations can be debatable—just ask Hollywood—it's nevertheless important for authors to use the ratings as a guide to review the content of their work. You don't want your book or story excluded from a potential audience because of one particular scene. If this quandary arises, it's best to look back at the scene and see if the narrative truly necessitates the level of description employed. If not then the scene is gratuitous and can either be edited, revised, or reconsidered in whole.

Dialog and language

The last concern on this subject is the use of graphic or expletive language in character dialog or narration. In the section on Writing Dialog, we looked at various ways to embody a character's voice through the character's spoken word and the considerations of extraneous dialog. It serves well to point out invocations from a character's perspective still fall under the cautions of gratuitous material.

As with many things, a good way to judge literary practice is to extrapolate from real world situations. In life, language and reaction that's laden with expletives fail to convey any constructive message. Typically, once people start throwing verbal bombs, bystanders only hear the bombs. Remember that even in dialog the message of the text should make the impact, not the extraneous "descriptive" language. There are times when a well-placed expletive can hammer home a character reaction without having to break from dialog into a narrative description. Be aware, however, that in most cases realistic dialog construction can convey a character's temperament without expletives.

☀

THE EXTENT OF RELEVANT EXPLICIT material within a story will vary upon author preference, story atmosphere, and the intended audience. Within these three considerations, keep in mind whether or not the material is required for each specific instance. That's not to say that a narrative or style has to be watered down, but more so that an author shouldn't bruise readers with said style or narrative construction.

For example consider if I had called this section "Working with f*****g explicit material." Such usage has no constructive effect. In fact it's nothing more than a distraction from the actual meaningful content of the section—and that, at the end of the day, should be an author's one concern when dealing with explicit material.

Developing your narrative voice

ONE OF THE HALLMARKS IN an author's maturation is the development of a unique narrative voice. This isn't to be confused with narrative perspective.

In the simplest of definitions, an author's narrative voice is the distinct sound and flow of an author's written work. This transcends narrative perspective, character personas, and subject matter so that an author's voice should identify his or her work no matter the nature of a given piece. In the world of literature, there's an old saying that every good story has already been told; the job of an author is to tell a story in a way unique to that author.

It's a concept that can be confusing for those who have only just started writing, because the natural response is to think, "Well, I wrote it, so of course it's mine." Narrative voice goes beyond putting your name under the title of a story. It's the product of experience through the labor of writing; it's something everyone has but requires time and patience to summon into words.

For those first dabbling in writing, the tricky process of understanding proper grammar and narrative techniques can obscure the sound of their narrative voice. Once these fundamentals become second nature, an author can concentrate on how the story itself is presented. Perhaps the first and most sure sign of an author recognizing his or her voice is with one simple thought when reading a book or story from another author. It goes like this: "That was interesting, but that's not how I would've written it." Rather than a criticism or egotistical claim, it's the recognition within authors of their particular brand of storytelling.

Amorphous and perhaps ambiguous a concept as it may be, narrative voice is a critical juncture in an author's writing life. Without this creative facet an author's work can be labeled as derivative. For sure it's an unwelcome term and something that readers and reviewers will detect while reading a particular story or book. A story that feels familiar yet is told with a distinctive voice will have more *lasting* impact on readers than a story told with an unremarkable voice.

The maturation of good narrative style and the development of a distinct narrative voice go hand in hand. Just as it's difficult to have a voice resonate in prose that hiccups with technical deficiencies, it's difficult for technically proficient prose to impact a reader if it lacks the author's unique voice. There's a certain irony that dwells within this process; then again, perhaps paradox is a better description.

While it's self-evident that the actual words of a story are everything to a reader, at the same time the writing itself should be transparent. Remember that the actual writing is a means to convey readers into the tale the author presents. Readers should at once be captivated by the structure of the prose at the same time that it flows almost unseen through their imagination. Although this may have the sound of flowery philosophy, or leave the impression that such concerns are more for poets than authors of prose, it is nevertheless the mark of an author who has come to inhabit his or her writing. It can even be said that this level of writing is what separates generic writing from something called literature in which the very expression of the written word is an artistic process in its own right.

Remember that readers are drawn to authors much the same way music fans are drawn to musicians, or movie fans are drawn to actors, directors, and screenwriters. People want and need to associate a particular experience with a creative source if they are to take interest in future works by that artist. Consider what makes creative performances distinctive: certain songs are unimaginable from any other musician, certain acting roles are inconceivable with any other actor in the part, and certain pieces of art are instantly recognizable as the work of a particular artist.

The same holds true for authors. As authors, when readers finish one of our written works, we want them to feel they've read something that couldn't have been told in the same way by any other author. It's how we, as artists in our own right, stake out our creative identity.

Everyone wants a fan base of readers. The best way for authors to build a lasting base is through their narrative voice.

PART 3

Regarding the Short Story Marketplace

"Hmm. I thought I'd write a book, but I think my idea fits better as a short story. So, what can I do with a short story?"

THE SHORT STORY MARKETPLACE IS a great opportunity for beginning authors to gain an understanding of the publishing world, build their writing credentials, learn from editors, sharpen editorial and writing skills, and earn some confidence. Like many authors it's where I first established my publishing footprint, and the lessons I learned along the way were invaluable when it was time to graduate to the world of books. In hindsight I can't imagine entering the book world without the experiences I had from this portion of the market.

To that end, we'll look at the following topics:

- Before sending out that first submission…
- Not every word is sacred
- Respect the playing field
- A word about query/cover letters
- Manuscript formats
- Word counts and story lengths
- Selecting markets
- Time to submit: a final checklist
- Evaluating editorial comments

The short story marketplace is a diverse and dynamic environment. Fledgling publications come and go on a regular basis, and there are small publications only seen by a handful of people. While a publication credit is a credit indeed, it's nice to know that somebody is actually going to read the published story. There are also larger, well-respected publications that can pay handsomely for accepted stories, but these are very difficult markets that accept less than one percent of the thousands of submissions they receive each *month*.

There are a number of things that should be considered when researching a publication for submission. The first and most obvious is to read the submission instructions from the editorial board. Second is to look over some of the previously published stories to see what kind of material the editors prefer to publish. Third is more a set of cautions: be wary of markets that publish poorly edited material, that have very small reader bases, and that don't publish on a regular basis, particularly if they haven't published anything recently or have gone off a stated publication schedule. The Internet has vastly increased the number of markets for short stories, but the sad reality is that some of these publication sites are abandoned.

It's very important to understand the economic realities under which short story publications exist. While the larger journals are viable business entities in their own right, many of the smaller publications, and certainly some of the university publications, are run as side projects by their staff. Independent publications are often the passion project of a handful of people who most likely have jobs and families aside from their literary interest. Sound familiar to many authors? At the university presses, the staff is often composed of a variety of students, graduate students, professors of various literary areas, and in some cases respected authors as honorary editorial staff members.

No matter the composition of the publication's staff, keep in mind that all but a few of the largest publications can rapidly change what they will and will not accept or if they will accept submissions at all. Given that most publications have a small set of readers to review submissions, it's not uncommon for publications to close their submissions for weeks or even months. University publications in particular are part of this reality, as they operate around their semester schedules. Some of these publications will allow submissions during off-semester times with the understanding that they won't be read until the semester reopens, while other publications will simply close their submissions.

One of the fortunate aspects of the Internet is that many publications have shifted away from paper submissions to electronic submissions. This not only saves trees but saves on postage as well. Electronic submissions can be done through email, proprietary uploads, or submission managers. Submission managers are a handy resource, as many contain progress notes on the status of a submission and may even contain editorial notes on a rejected submission.

If a publication is still doing things the old-fashioned way with paper submissions, remember proper postal mail etiquette. That is to say, *follow the submission instructions*. I'll talk more about this later, but one important thing to know right from the beginning is to *never* send a short story postal submission with a return receipt request. It's a sure way for your submission to be rejected without being opened.

Ready to go? Great—but not so fast. A little forethought when approaching the short story marketplace can make your efforts more efficient and effective.

Before sending out that first submission …

Organization is a critical part of the short story process not often addressed in author guides. Given that the average short story endures roughly forty rejections and two years of submission wait times, the idea of sending out one story at a time and waiting is simply unrealistic. Following that submission model might entail a long wait before anything sees the light of day.

The great advantage of working with short stories is just that—the plurality of submissions. Whereas submissions in the book world operate on a very different time scale due to the size of work to be considered, short story submissions can be optimized to make the most of your time in researching where to send your stories. There will be more detail about selecting markets later in this part. For now let's take a look at the basics of the short story submission process.

An individual journal or magazine is considered a *market*. Every market will have a set of instructions for submissions, generated by the editorial staff. These guides can be found with the greatest ease—and will be the most up to date—at the market's website. The standard set of submission instructions will list the genres considered by the market, acceptable word lengths, submission periods, requested copyright terms upon publication acceptance, typical submission response times, method of submission—postal mail, email, submission manager, etc.—payment rate, if any, and any additional specific instructions. Whether you do your market research through one of the printed guidebooks available in book stores, or you rely completely on the Internet for your searches, you must understand your target market's submission instructions before you send off a story.

The most significant variance between markets is whether or not they accept simultaneous submissions. *Simultaneous submissions* entail the process where the target market understands the story may be submitted to several markets at once. When submitting to these markets, understand that it's the author's professional responsibility to send withdrawal notifications to the pending markets should the story get accepted for publication. Editors will not respond kindly if they spend the time considering a short story only to discover the author already agreed to publication in another market.

While it's tempting to blanket the short story market with simultaneous submissions for a particular story, it's best to refrain from this practice. Known as a *blitz,* this can backfire. As exciting as it may be to have two or more editors send acceptance notifications for a story, and even though editors understand that authors may have to choose between acceptance letters *on occasion,* editors are also very much aware of the reality of submissions. Editors who accept simultaneous submissions play the odds; as industry insiders they know full well the success rate of any submission is minute at best. In practice it is in fact quite unlikely that a story will receive acceptance from two or more publications at once. Once again be considerate and conscious of the time editors invest in the submission and acceptance process.

A final consideration for simultaneous submissions is the revision process. It's important to understand that the majority of publications print a submission in the form it was sent to them. After all, they've judged it acceptable in the form they've seen. Unless an editor asks for revisions, it's poor etiquette to respond to an acceptance letter by saying that you have a newer, revised version of the story. In fact this may lead to the acceptance being withdrawn. While you as the author are thinking, "I have an even better version of the story," the editor is going to think, "Great, now I have to re-evaluate this submission because I'm not overworked enough."

Part of this understanding is that some editors who reject a submission will offer a critique or editorial comment on the story to help the author improve its quality. If the story is a simultaneous submission strewn across many markets, the author loses the opportunity to offer those markets what could be a better version in the wake of editorial input. This is important to note because some publications track *all* the submissions they receive—particularly those who utilize a submission manager. Unless an editor has specifically requested a revision as part of the acceptance process, editors will often spontaneously reject a resubmitted title.

Non-simultaneous submissions mean the target market will only consider material on an exclusive basis. There's an honor system here of course. Remember that when an author submits to a publication, he/ she is already entering into a professional arrangement, informal as it may be. Considering that if the market accepts an author's story it will satisfy its end of the deal through publication, playing by the rules of exclusivity is a small commitment on the author's part. The long and short is that if an author wants to submit to a non-simultaneous market, then patience is required to wait through the response period. The good news is that rejections often come very quickly—sometimes in hours—whereas acceptance notifications take time.

It's best to approach the short story marketplace with a stable of stories. This provides a great deal of flexibility and if a number of submissions are out at once, overall wait times for potential publication may decrease. When my publication focus was on short stories, I looked to keep at least four or five submissions going at any one time for each short story I was looking to publish. If I decided to do a revision on a given story, I would wait until my current submissions were answered before sending out a new batch of submissions. I also submitted on rolling periods, so that I staggered markets with faster response times between markets with longer response times.

When working with a number of stories, it's easy to get lost in the submission process. Organization is a key factor when sending out multiple stories to multiple markets. The most basic model for organization is to take a blank sheet of paper for each story and keep a written record of the story's submissions. Divide the page into columns for the name of the market, date submitted, how submitted—postal mail, email, submission manager—expected response time, and response result. Leave space for various notes, such as whether or not it was a paying market, if it participates in award programs, and most notably if it had a non-simultaneous submission policy.

In the world of computers, of course, paper records are antiquated. Spreadsheets are a much more powerful tool. For most people that will mean using Microsoft Excel, but any spreadsheet program will do. With one file, in a single view, you can manage all of your submissions.

There are different ways to format such a file. When in doubt, keep it simple:

1. Across the head of the page create columns for each story. Beneath each story include the word count, as this is important for eligibility in different markets.
2. Down the left side of the page list markets in alphabetical order with a small note of S for simultaneous submissions or NS for non-simultaneous submissions.
3. On the far right of the page, keep an informal record of your publications, including story, publication date, and word count. Aside from keeping record of what markets granted you publication, it helps act as a positive reinforcement.

With such a file, tracking submissions is simply a matter of cross-referencing a market and a story. When submitting, enter the submission date in the corresponding cell and color it yellow. When a rejection comes in, change the cell entry to *Rejected* and color the cell pink Personally, I always feel red seems too angry. If a market replies with an acceptance, send email withdrawals to any markets that are yet to respond for that story, then delete the story's column and add an entry to the publication record.

For a more refined system, consider either color-coding the markets or adding letter codes to denote what genres of stories they consider. This can be helpful if you plan to work with stories across a wide subject or genre spectrum. Using such a system, and working with several stories, it's not unrealistic to have twenty or more pending submissions at once.

Not every word is sacred

ANYONE WHO HAS TAKEN THE effort to write fiction will be familiar with the emotional investment required to put words to paper, so to speak. As such, there's a natural inclination to feel that stories as originally told shouldn't be altered in any significant way. This transcends concerns of simple grammar edits, proofreads, and content edit to question the entirety of a piece of fiction. As a rule authors feel that their stories are their "babies."

In Part 2, Basic Writing Mechanics, we took a look at editorial processes. This section is more about reviewing a story and learning how to judge if it works or needs improvement—thereby the adage, "not every word is sacred."

There's another little adage that the process of revision is endless. A common dilemma for authors is deciding when to end the revision process and start the submission process. By nature it's a very subjective decision and one that will be easier to delineate as experience builds confidence in both an author's writing and editing abilities. There's hardly an author out there who doesn't feel one more proofing could find something to give a story an extra tweak of improvement. Hindsight, as they say, is twenty-twenty.

As an author be ready to look back at your stories and revise in stages. One of my published stories, "Memento," went through a series of revisions before I had the story in the form I desired. Though it had accumulated a number of rejections with its earlier versions, the last revision found its acceptance with *Reed Magazine* rather quickly. This process was a lesson in itself. When I started sending the story out for consideration in its original form, I believed it was the best it could be. As the story built up its track of rejections, I took a much more *objective* look at the story and dispensed with my *subjective* affection for the original form. Once I was able to make that switch in perspective, the revision gained both scope and momentum, and *voila*, the story was accepted.

The point is that revising a story is an evolutionary process. A story may seem just right, but if it isn't hitting the mark of publication, it may be time to consider further critique. This brings forth a gem of advice that floats around author circles: after writing a story and performing the nuts-and-bolts editorial process, let the story sit for some time. This will allow for several things.

First, it provides a vital sense of emotional distance. During the writing process, it can be very difficult for an author to separate from the innate awareness of the story's totality. This can lead to erroneous assumptions regarding narrative facets that may escape the reader. It can also create a flaw in the story's emotional arc. Allowing the story to sit dissipates an author's inner awareness of the narrative so that the story can be read closer to the perspective of a reader.

Second, after the story sits it will be easier to critique overall narrative structure. Maybe there's a word used in repetition, a certain phrase that comes too often from different characters, or descriptive passages that aren't necessary. It's much easier to perform this type of narrative problem solving without the clutter of the story's emotional hold over editorial judgment.

Third, consider how interesting the story is during a read. The support of beta readers can be indispensable in this phase, but it can be done on your own using one simple rule of judgment. If you, as the author, don't feel captivated by the story—if you don't feel the same "magic" as when you wrote the story—it's a safe bet the reader won't feel it either. Once the story isn't as intimate to you as when first created, you can ask if you indeed told something new, compelling, or captivating enough to hold an audience.

In the end it's your story. That won't change, no matter how many revisions.

Respect the playing field

IT MAY SEEM LIKE A broken record to stress the importance of technical writing skills, but once again, it's crucial to ensure your grammar is in good shape when sending out a story. While this step will be performed prior to greater concerns of revision, it should always be the final step before considering submission. Remember, a story won't hold an editor's attention if it contains too many spelling and grammar errors.

To give another broken record its due, remember that while you may be sending out your story as a hobby or a passionate side pursuit, publication is a *profession* to many editors and reading panels of magazines, journals, and/or literary agencies. As such, approach your submission target not as an artistic foray but as a professional interaction. Basic spelling, typing, and grammar constitute the best way to say to a reviewing reader that you are at least serious and respectful of the business of writing. Editors are there to consider the value of your storytelling, not to teach you lessons in basic English.

No matter what you submit or where you submit, there will always be submission guidelines. Like the basic mechanics of writing, failure to respect the rules of an editor's guidelines is a good way to torpedo a submission.

At minimum your work should be neat, printed on one side of a page, double-spaced, and contain in the query letter and/or in the story itself your contact information. If editors have more individualized requirements, it's best to follow them. Thanks to the Internet, many publications have web sites detailing current submission guidelines. If a specific editor is named for a genre of interest, address the submission to that editor. This minor attention to detail will already help separate your submission from the masses of blank submissions.

Once again, be mindful as to which publications will accept simultaneous submissions and those that will not. It's considered good submission etiquette to denote in the cover letter whether or not a story is part of a simultaneous submission.

By now the topic of cover letters has come up several times. Time for another opportune segue ...

A word about query/cover letters

Whether submitting via email, submission manager, proprietary upload, or postal mail, a vital part of the submission package is the query or cover letter. Consider this letter your professional introduction to an editor.

As important as a good cover letter can be, cover letters often face a mixed fate. There are some opinions that cover letters are a waste of time and serve as nothing more than vanity notes from authors to be disposed by editors or review readers. At the other end of the spectrum, there are those editors and review readers who say their first opinion on the fate of a submission comes with the impression of the cover letter. A poorly written letter, like a poorly written resume for a job application, won't speak well for the submitted story. In fact there are editors and review readers who openly state that a poorly executed cover letter will doom a submission without being read. How large a percentage of the submission audience holds this practice is open to question, and therein once more resides the importance of the cover letter.

In short a cover letter can only help, not hurt, except for the occasional editor who specifies not to send a cover letter. What helps make a good cover letter? Here's a brief checklist:

1. Be sure to address the letter to the specific editor for your submission, if one is noted in the submission instructions for the particular publication.
2. First paragraph should be straight to the point: the title of the story, the word count, and the genre. Unless instructed to do so, *do not* summarize the story.
3. Second paragraph can contain publication credits and awards. It isn't necessary to list every achievement. If your credentials are lengthy, mention those that are most notable and/or most relevant to the publication you are targeting. For example, if it's a mystery magazine and you've published a mystery story, most certainly mention this foremost among your credentials.
4. Third paragraph can contain a short bio, two or three sentences at the most.

5. In closing you must note whether the story is a simultaneous submission or not. Some opinions state that editors with these respective policies will assume that you, as the submitting author, understand the difference. There are other editors, however, who state that if this isn't specified in the case of a non-simultaneous submission policy, the submission will be rejected unread. Either way it seems a simple courtesy to include this notation and a simple way to show an editor that you did in fact read the submission guidelines.

6. Thoroughly spell and grammar check the cover letter.

7. Once the cover letter is the best it can be, keep two versions: one with an author bio and one without, as this is the most common variance in editorial instructions for cover letters. With these two files complete, they can be sent in print, or copied and pasted into emails and submission managers. As you earn your publication credentials, be sure to update the letter, even with pending publication dates. It's in your favor to present yourself as an active participant in the marketplace.

Manuscript formats

AFTER A COVER LETTER, HOW you present your story is the first introduction of your writing to an editor. Just as how you dress is important when you walk into an interview, so too the proper formatting of your story is important when an editor gives it a look.

We'll look at the three most common standards: universal formatting, *standard* formatting, and online or "web" formatting.

Universal Formatting

These are the basic parameters by which every story should abide when sent out. Some of them may sound ridiculous, but some people do strange things. After all there wouldn't be warning stickers about storing gas cans next to open fires if someone hadn't tried.

1. Always double-space.
2. Do not send handwritten work.
3. Print on one side of the page.
4. Left margin; do not justify margins.

5. Use 12 pt., Times New Roman font.
6. For new paragraphs, set a standard indentation of five spaces either with a tab or a paragraph format function.
7. Contact information on first page.
8. Header information with your name, story title, and page number.
9. If submitting by Internet, be sure to submit the requested file type: *.doc, *.rtf, or email paste.
10. If submitting by postal mail, don't forget to include a good old SASE for editorial reply.

What's an SASE? Self-Addressed, Stamped Envelope.

Standard Formatting

This is in addition to, or in place of, the above. Don't get confused—it's easy to mistake what a *standard* format is until checking what it entails. Standard formatting is something you may encounter when submitting to genre publications, such as science fiction, horror, and fantasy.

1. Use Courier, the font that looks like old typewriter print.
2. Contact information at top left of first page, word count at top right.
3. Approximately half way down first page, list story title, next line put "by," next line your name, all centered.
4. Page header, top right, with your last name/story title/page number.
5. Denote scene breaks with a single centered asterisk.
6. Do not use italics. Denote text that is to be italicized by underlining the text, excepting editor permission.
7. At story end, leave a few blank lines, and then type THE END, centered.

Online Formatting

This is something that may be difficult to appreciate unless one has worked with websites. Online formatting was born from the differences of format code between word processors and HTML, the computer language of the Internet. If you submit to online publications and you see the specification for online or "web" formatting, be sure to follow these guidelines.

1. Within paragraphs, single-space. NO hard returns.
2. Use a hard return between paragraphs. In HTML this will convert to a blank line between paragraphs.
3. Denote scene breaks with three centered asterisks.
4. Do not use a double space after a period; follow with only a single space.
5. In some cases it will be requested that paragraph indents be omitted.

OF COURSE, AS SHOULD GO without saying, *always follow the submission guidelines* that editors lay out for their publications. There are some editors with more specific guidelines, and even a few with unique guidelines, that if neglected can doom a submission.

Word counts and story length

ASIDE FROM A SHORT STORY's genre, the most significant technical aspect of short story markets rests on the word count of a story. Any word processor has a tool to provide a word count; for publication purposes the count should be rounded to the nearest five hundred or thousand, such as 5,000 or 5,500 words. Listing a word count as 5,374 words is a sure tip-off that the submission is from a beginner. While this won't condemn a piece, it may predispose an editor or review reader to the opinion that they are dealing with someone less than professional.

There's a definitive market perspective on story length. For the purpose of a general discussion, 5,000 words is the magic threshold in the short story marketplace. The majority of publications—both web and print—will consider stories below this count. Once a story crosses the 5,000-word cap, the number of publications drops by at least half. There's another big reduction in available markets after the 8,000-word mark. If a story surpasses the 10,000-word mark, the number of available markets is quite small. Remember that increased story length entails a correspondingly larger space commitment within an issue, regardless of whether the publication is electronic or print.

Consider as well that most editors look to provide their readers with a spectrum of fiction in a given issue. In quite a number of publications, issues are devoted to a particular theme; in others there are more understated thematic links. Nevertheless, a thematically linked issue—no matter how subtle the link—will draw part of its strength from the diversity of its contents. For an issue to commit to a lengthy story isn't just a matter of editorial risk on one story, but a risk of casting a particular light on the issue itself.

These concerns will vary depending on the individual constitution and editorial preferences of a given publication, but these factors contribute to understanding why longer pieces of fiction have so many fewer publications willing to entertain them.

Now, with that said, the second consideration on story length naturally comes in the actual writing of the story. Different writers have different views on this subject, particularly with writing being such an individualized exercise. As an overall recommendation, don't worry so much about length or word count during the writing process. I for one do not write my stories following an outline; on the contrary I tend to have a general idea where I want to go with my story and then let my character development decide on the complexity, and therefore the length, of the piece. Aside from this personal inclination, a good rule of thumb is that a story encompasses a length required for the character(s) to complete the intended emotional arc of the story. Remember, for a reader to be emotionally invested in a story, the characters must be emotionally invested.

With a little bit of planning and thought, extraneous scenes can be avoided during the writing process; proofreading will reveal other areas of the piece that can be trimmed down or, if necessary, expanded. A general tip for maintaining momentum, and by extension controlling word count, is that your reader should never be wondering when something is going to "happen."

Consider how many characters you want to work with, the complexity of your story idea, and what may be required to relate your idea to readers. All these concerns will combine ahead of time to give a rough idea of a story's potential length. That said, be cautious of taking a story that has received a great deal of proofing and then "chopping" it to make it fit under a certain word count.

There's always a happy medium between the momentum of a story and its length. When these sometimes opposing factors are out of balance, a story will either drag or feel incomplete. It's not an easy balance to achieve, and each story will have its own point of compromise. In the end remember that as story length increases, the market availability decreases.

With all this in mind, here are some guidelines on story lengths:

- *500 - 1,000 (or <500):* Considered *flash fiction*. Good market availability for submissions.
- *Up to 5,000:* Considered *short* story. This is the main segment of the market, so excellent availability for submissions.
- *5,000 - 8,000:* Still in the short story realm, but significantly less markets available for submissions.
- *8,000 - 10,000:* The high end of the short story realm, few markets available for submissions.
- *>10,000:* Entering the realm of novellas. Very few markets available; the best bet is to submit to anthologies.
- *20,000 - 70,000:* A tough area between long novellas, "novelettes," and short novels. Even when submitting to an anthology, this is a major commitment for an editor and so a tough sell. If you have several stories of this length, consider any common elements between them and group them into an anthology.
- *>70,000:* Congratulations! You didn't write a story, you wrote a book. Humor aside, definitions vary by publisher, but in most cases word counts in this range are the realm of full length, stand-alone novels.

Selecting markets

THE STORY IS WRITTEN, PROPERLY formatted, and the cover letter is ready to go—now what?

It's time to select your markets.

The best advice for this process comes in three words: research, research, research. Seeking publication is a tedious, time-consuming process. Even if that first publication credit comes after a few submissions, don't be fooled into thinking publication will get any easier. To once again repeat a sobering set of statistics, the average short story goes through forty rejections and two years of time before finding its home in a publication. During the search for publication, it's not uncommon to have some stories place ahead of that curve and a few that go beyond; ergo, the reality of the curve.

Given the subjective nature of story acceptance, there's little to do beyond making sure the submission is properly edited, revised, and presented other than looking to see if the story is a good fit for the target market. Even with that variable addressed, there's no guarantee. So with research, research, research, goes patience, perseverance, more patience, and some more perseverance.

There are many reference books out there, and of course there's the Internet. Two great sites are Ralan.com and Duotrope.com, and the gold standard in print is the annual short story reference from Writer's Market. Print and Internet sources don't necessarily overlap, so it's best to use both in building lists of possible markets for your stories. Regardless of where you reference a market, follow up on the Internet when possible to get the most current submission information.

A publication's archives are most often the best indicator of how appropriate the market is for your particular submission. If these archives are available online, it's of great benefit to read or skim at least a few of the recently published stories. The focus should be on recent issues to ensure back-issue availability—in the event the market publishes your story—and to ensure you're submitting to the same staff of editors and review readers. Publications can change their staff without notice, either as part of an effort to revitalize or to simply pursue a different literary direction. These changes can have marked effects on the complexion of accepted submissions.

Once again pay close attention to the submission guidelines where most editors will make it quite clear what kind of material they consider. Remember that these instructions often summarize an editor's battle scars from wading through submission slush piles. When I started sending out stories, I was amazed how many editors actually specified they wouldn't accept handwritten submissions *in crayon*. The first time I read this I thought someone had sipped an extra shot of sarcasm juice, but I've read several editorial columns claiming this actually happens. Other gaffes on the hit list of editors consist of submissions sent on fancy paper, colored paper, printed in various or non-standard fonts, fancy bindings, and even submissions written in calligraphy.

These obvious miscues aside, there will be times when it's difficult to get a thorough feel for an editor's exact tastes. There are those who say their tastes are "eclectic," which can be a particularly tough description to unravel. Aside from reading archived stories, submitting to such markets might have to be done on a wing and a prayer. In the end, though, the best bet is to use common sense. A publication website that has flowery pages and images of unicorns, but states eclectic editorial tastes, won't be interested in a grisly horror story, no matter how spectacular.

It's important to maintain a wide focus, by which is meant not to fixate on a particular market. There will be publications whose guidelines or back issues seem to fall along the similar lines of a particular planned submission. This may lead you to think, "Wow, my story is perfect for these guys!" The truth is that there are probably a few hundred, or even a few thousand, authors thinking the same exact thing—for that month alone.

When submitting, be sure to review the rights exchanged for submission; specifically, which part of your copyright will be ceded to the publication for the story's acceptance. The standard among markets in the United States is FNASR, or First North American Serial Rights. This clause allows the market to be the first to secure publication rights for North America. The implication of this agreement is the author's validation that the story hasn't been published in any form. Remember that a story posted on a blog or any other source is considered published. For online markets, the clause will be along the lines of first worldwide digital or electronic publication.

Whatever the media in which the story will appear, be certain that no lasting hold will remain on the story. Reputable publications let all rights revert to the author some time after publication, usually six to twelve months. Any other terms, or lack of specificity on terms, should be cause for further consideration. There are a few markets that try to exert eternal holds on their published material, and these markets will require a great deal of deliberation on the part of the author as to whether or not to submit.

Competition might seem like a dirty word when considering an artistic pursuit such as writing and publication, but it is indeed competitive. A submitted story has to stand on its own against many other submissions to receive a full initial read. From there it may have to survive two or more successive editorial reviews before being accepted for publication. Some market references contain quotes as to submission rates for different markets. There's no hard and fast rule for how discriminating a market may be; indeed, some fledgling publications only accept a tiny fraction of their submissions. The reality is that there are far more authors and submissions than all markets combined can publish.

Despite the challenge of securing that first acceptance letter—and any others that follow—remember that each publication credit is a success. Any submission is stacked against very high odds, so every acceptance is a moment to celebrate.

Time to submit: a final checklist

It's best to run through a final checklist of items before sending out a submission. After all the time spent writing, editing, and researching, a few extra minutes of attention won't hurt. There's no greater frustration than discovering some small but vital mistake after sending out a round of submissions.

Here's a quick checklist to evaluate the readiness of a submission:

1. In the most objective view, is the story the best it can be?
2. Have you run a final spell and grammar check to catch any small errors, particularly if the story just underwent an edit or revision?
3. Did you generate a word count from your word processor and identify your story's genre?
4. Determine your target market(s) and delineate between simultaneous and non-simultaneous.

5. Is the market open to submissions at this time?
6. Double check story manuscript for formatting as required by submission instructions.
7. Double check cover letter, making sure to use correct publication/editor addressee.
8. Note response time, type of submission—postal, electronic, simultaneous, etc.—in your records.

Evaluating editorial comments

Given the volume of submissions sent to publications, it's often difficult, if not impossible, for editors to supply comments on rejections. When comments do come, they should be given careful consideration. On the other hand, this doesn't mean they should be taken as absolute. Editorial critique can fall into two categories, the objective and the subjective.

Objective criticism

Critique of this nature concerns the technical structure and approach to the story, and constitutes the typical sources of editorial criticism. It's often difficult for authors to maintain objective scrutiny of a story, given their intimacy to its creation. In the realm of short stories, editorial comments are to the point. For those coming into the publishing world from outside academic circles and degrees in creative writing, these objective comments can be priceless. Even if you disagree with the comment, use it to consider what facet of the story could inspire a misinterpretation of the intended goal.

Subjective criticism

Comments from this perspective regard an editor's emotional reaction to the piece, most often whether or not the piece successfully grabbed the editor's attention or is a proper fit for the publication in question. Being subjective, these editorial comments are not absolute. As with certain objective criticisms, consider subjective comments with respect to the story you wanted to present.

Comments of this nature can be brushed off in a beginning author's belief that the editor simply "didn't get" the story. Consider, however, that editors see thousands of stories. If an editor missed what a story was meant to convey, perhaps the problem isn't with the message *per se*, but only the way in which it was delivered. At this level subjective comments can become more like objective comments because they dwell within the story structure itself. Either way it's a situation that can be fixed.

☀

OBJECTIVE OR SUBJECTIVE, REMEMBER THAT any comment stems from how the story was interpreted by an experienced reader. Whether agreeing with the comment or not, give it careful thought. It may lead you to see something of which you were previously unaware, or perhaps even make you conscious of an element in the story you had not fully considered.

On a personal note, I've had the fortune to experience a number of editorial comments in my short story endeavors. Of those comments there was only one that I rejected on its face because the editor went on at length as to how the story should be written—in effect, the editor wanted to shadow-write my story. I mention this to illustrate an important point. The exchange between editor and author is directly analogous to coach and athlete. Just as the coach stays on the sideline while pushing the athlete to be better, so too the editor coaxes the best out of an author without replacing the author.

All the other comments I've received were both helpful and welcome. The fact that an editor took time to offer what is essentially free advice not only showed a commitment to the art of writing but a concern for my particular story. In the cases where I received editorial comment as part of a rejection, I was naturally disappointed over the rejection but happy to receive the comment.

For one of my stories, "Beheld," this was a crucial experience. The story was written with abstract and philosophical extents and staged on a grand scale. What I didn't realize it lacked—until one editor pointed it out—was that while the story had good merits, it had no dramatic resolution within the narrative. As such, it was an interesting *essay*, but not a *story*. In all the attention I invested on its higher points, I missed this fundamental aspect. Aided by this comment, I went back to the story, worked through a minor revision, and soon afterward it was accepted and published.

PART 4

Regarding Novels

"Phew, my story idea turned into a whole book. Forget short stories, I need to figure out what to do on a whole new level. So what can I do with a book?"

THAT'S THE BIGGEST QUESTION IN the book world. In this section we'll take a look at the differences between publishers, examine some of the technicalities of book production, delve various considerations to provide a basic understanding of the book market, and prepare book submission materials. After, we'll take a look at a few fundamental steps you can take in the transition from publishing to marketing. So to that end we'll move through the following topics:

- A brief history of self-, small, and large publishers
- The big question: self-, small, or large publisher
- How large publishers leverage books to win in the marketplace
- Book economics: price points, expenses, and royalties
- Considerations for book design
- Considerations for book length
- Distribution acronyms: ISBN, ASIN, UPC, EAN and LCCN
- Book production services
- A few words on audiobooks
- Literary agents: some pros and cons
- Preparing a book submission/query package
- The book is published—now what?
- Considerations for book reviews: a first step after publication
- Be brave—enter an award contest!
- A bigger picture: have your own publishing imprint
- Summation: the book world, in a nutshell

As interesting, challenging, and educational as pursuits can be in the short story marketplace, the bulk of the publishing industry centers on books. It's a rare author indeed who can make a steady income from short story publication, given that the vast majority of markets don't pay. This isn't to say that achieving publication with a book will land one in a pot of gold. Ask many authors and the answer will be surprising. The economic reality of the book world is that a small handful of authors realize the lion's share of book sales. The remaining percentage of the overall book market is divided into precipitous tiers of diminishing returns, with the clear majority of authors realizing no more than perhaps a sale or two per month. With hundreds of thousands of titles published *each year* in the United States alone, this shouldn't be a surprise.

Very few books enter the marketplace with the required marketing and publicity muscle to spur significant initial sales. Large publishers open doors to these services, but for the most part the expenses are considered the author's responsibility. For all the other authors with publishers of varying smaller scales, and those who are self-published, the success of their books will depend on the dogged pursuit of affordable, practical marketing measures and a large dose of perseverance.

The single biggest obstacle for a book's success is the author's gumption to champion his or her own writing. This is particularly true for those who publish only one book. Too many books flounder and vanish from perception because the author either didn't know how to market or was demoralized by the scale of the marketing learning curve. When it comes to marketing there's a great debate as to how it ties to an author's publisher, the scale of the publisher, and the relevance of social networking.

With that in mind we'll take a look at different levels of publishers, how the book market has shaped to its current form, what it means to prospective authors, and different approaches an author can take to build initial awareness of a title. When it comes to discussions of publishers, it's inevitable to discuss marketing. While this part will dip a toe in those waters, they'll be explored in greater depth in Part 5, Regarding Marketing.

A brief history of self-, small, and large publishers

To MANY PEOPLE OUTSIDE OF the publishing industry, it might appear that the current diversity among publishers is a recent development spurred by the boon of self-publishing. While the publishing landscape has certainly changed, the truth is that there's always been an amalgam of publishers.

Major publishers have dominated the marketplace for decades and arguably continue to do so today. In the past, however, there were more rigid separations between the various levels of publishers. Major publishers were most notable for their extensive partnerships with book distribution chains. In the days before print-on-demand technology and the ever-present Internet, books were only available through a handful of large distributors taking orders from bookstores and libraries. Major publishers put this network to their best use, and their sheer scale allowed them to leverage large print runs of popular titles against less popular or recognizable authors.

While the Internet has had a huge impact on the publishing business, particularly in the form of electronic books, perhaps of equal or greater impact has been the advent of print-on-demand technology. This has changed the game for many smaller publishers and, without doubt, revolutionized the model of self-publishers. To understand this change it helps to understand how the traditional book business model worked—and, for the top-tier authors of major publishers, continues to work to this day.

In the traditional publishing model, books are manufactured in print runs. The numeric size and distribution of the print run is in relation to the publisher's expectation as to the book's commercial performance. Successful authors receive larger runs, while less known authors receive smaller runs; likewise, titles expected to have strong sales receive large runs while smaller titles receive smaller runs. This is a somewhat tricky process because a print run embodies a business risk in material expense. The books are printed, stored, distributed, and the costs absorbed in expectation the run will sell enough copies to turn profitable.

Success of the first print run is crucial to a title's future. If the first run experiences poor sales, the second run can be much smaller or canceled altogether. Hardcover print runs are often reserved for titles considered as safe sales bets, given the much higher manufacturing cost. For a book to continue into repeated print runs requires continued profitable sales figures. The catch to this process, however, is that a print run requires time since it involves a material manufacturing process. Print runs are also done on cycles that may not correspond with a demand spike for a particular title.

From the author's perspective, royalty rates are scaled with the number of print runs; that is, the typical publishing deal involves the potential for a set number of print runs with increasing royalty rates on each successive run. At the end of the publishing deal, rates can then be renegotiated for additional runs.

In the past the financial overhead of a print run constituted a business risk that smaller publishers often found difficult to sustain. In the old days of publishing, the typical smaller presses were either university presses or so-called "vanity" presses. We'll take a look at vanity presses in a moment.

University presses exist in their own realm. Some of these presses are now imprints—subdivisions, in effect—operating under major publishers. University presses have profit centers in textbook sales, and anyone who's gone to college knows this game very well. There's a built-in sales demand due to the textbooks listed as requirements for various courses. Such books sell at exorbitant premiums and are then effectively devalued by the emergence of a "new" edition the next year. There has always been a murky zone in this business model where professors write the textbooks for the classes they teach.

Aside from textbooks, university presses also pride themselves as the source of what one could call "high" literature, the sort of material that circulates among inner circles of the literary elite but finds little market presence within the commercial book world.

Vanity presses received their somewhat derogatory title because of their business model. Whereas major publishers had their titles vetted through the process of agent acquisition and editorial selection, vanity presses offered authors a direct line to publication. Unfortunately, too many of these presses had little or no editorial quality control.

Their business model was geared toward one end, and that was to take payment from the author for a print run. It was for all purposes a pay-to-play model where the press deferred the cost risk of the run onto the author. The publisher charged the author for the basic book production costs and any editorial expense. In addition it was up to the author to swallow the cost of the actual print run. These runs often numbered a thousand books or higher, representing a material expense to the author of several thousand dollars. It was then upon the author's shoulders to sell the books. If this effort failed, the material loss fell upon the author, not the publisher. There are too many sad stories of eager authors tapping the service of a vanity publisher, only to end up with stacks of books growing mold in their garages.

This isn't to say, however, that all vanity presses subscribed to such practices. Indeed, one can say that the current boon of self-publishing wouldn't exist without a thriving, reputable core of small and self-publishers that exist unseen and often unrecognized beneath the gargantuan marketing muscle of the major publishers.

Print-on-demand technology was a game changer for the smaller scale publishers. Whereas the major publishers still rely on the print run model for many titles, publishers down the size chain have embraced print-on-demand. This technology revolutionized the business because it allowed for digitization of an entire book, which could then be printed in as many or few copies as needed at any moment. Unlike the old print run model, there's no need for the labor and expense of mechanical typesetting that is then disassembled after the run is manufactured. With print-on-demand, the old disreputable vanity model that compelled authors to plunk down large sums of money for dubious sales prospects has greatly diminished.

Together, the Internet and print-on-demand effectively opened the doors to publication for the masses. The cost curve for prospective authors to self-publish dropped drastically with the elimination of the print run expense; likewise, the business prospects for smaller publishers were much more amenable since the print run overhead was eliminated. Storage expenses, print run lead times, and a host of other business considerations lost relevance.

Ease of access did not translate to ease of sales, however. While small publishers saw their business models become more viable for them and their authors, it was the self-publishing segment of the market that experienced explosive growth. Digitization and instant access through the Internet sent untold numbers of prospective authors frustrated by the barriers of the agent/editor/major publisher model to seek self-publication.

Unfortunately, even though the old model could leave quality authors and books floundering for lack of subjective support, the open door of self-publishing eliminated the crucial vetting process intrinsic to the old model. As the number of self-published titles rapidly expanded, the traditional publishing market effectively closed ranks to what was often viewed as a tidal wave of poorly written, poorly edited, and cheaply produced books. Self-published titles were simply regarded as not good enough to find acceptance in the traditional model, and so were viewed with great skepticism.

These hurdles were still evident in 2010. I can say this because at that time I was researching publishers for my first book, *Remnant*, and I had to tackle the question of whether to seek out a small publisher or self-publish. Research provided a rather stark answer in the form of the black mark upon self-published titles. A tried and true way to establish a book's credibility is through professional reviews and awards. In 2010 it was hard to find a professional reviewing service or reputable award competition that would accept self-published titles. It was very much like the No Dogs Allowed sign thrust into a cute canine's face in old cartoons.

Like everything else digital, however, things changed rapidly. In 2012, when my second book, *Oddities & Entities*, was published, I was surprised as to how many review services and awards were not only open to self-published titles but in some cases had gone so far as to establish special categories for these titles. The cynical side of the market looked upon this as a simple business calculation by these venues to generate income from aspiring self-published authors, and the cynics would often point to those special self-publish categories as continued evidence that such titles weren't worthy of competing with vetted titles from the traditional publishing process.

Two factors indirectly led to change this perception: the growing realization that royalty rates for authors could be much different outside of traditional publishing and the advent of quality, reliable e-book devices such as the Kindle and Nook.

Royalty rates vary across the scale of publishers. Some newcomers to the market have the misconception that the highest rates are paid by the major publishers, when in fact the exact opposite is true. The common royalty rate for major publishers on a first run is roughly 5%, scaling upward depending on print runs, the commercial value of an author's name, and expected or proven sales. Even so, an 11% royalty rate from a major publisher is considered high. Moving down the size scale to smaller publishers, the royalty rate is often in the neighborhood of 40%. The difference lies in the distribution expectation of the major publishers. While small publishers might be ecstatic with a sales figure of several thousand copies, a major publisher is expecting sales of at least tens or hundreds of thousands. This offsets the decreased royalty.

Among self-publishers in today's world, royalty rates can be as high as 70%. It sounds very appetizing, but the catch for authors is to understand that royalties are irrelevant if books don't sell. What brought attention to this rate differential, though, was when A-list authors began turning out titles through self-publishers to realize a large increase in their royalty share. For such authors it was a very profitable move: they already possessed the priceless advantages of name recognition and established, widespread reader bases.

This led to some major publishers to cry foul, stating—and not too erroneously—that the very authors the publishers helped build were now jumping ship for more money. It's a volatile debate that transcends this discussion, but the outcome is important here. With A-list authors releasing new titles through self-publishers, attention was suddenly turned on the wide array of authors from both self- and small publishers. Lo and behold, there was a paradigm shift in market perceptions as many people began to discover the number of well-written and professionally produced books outside the major publishers. This in turn caused another explosive growth in the self- and small publishing segments, as they could now claim viable success stories and well-known authors in their publishing history.

It was a blow to the major publishers, but they responded in kind by embracing what they could no longer deny. Perhaps the most notable step in this direction was Penguin's acquisition of self-publishing giant Author House and all its imprints. Although some in the market considered this sacrilege, as the saying goes, money talks and something rather pungent walks. Since the Penguin deal, other major publishers have either established their own self-publish imprints or have acquired reputable self-publishers.

The phenomenon of e-books emerged as the market was swirling around the confluence of different publishers and the debate over royalty rates. Once Amazon figured a way to get its e-reading service and Kindle device coordinated in a similar manner as Apple found success with the coordination of its I-tunes store and I-pod devices, the market wouldn't be the same again. The flexibility of self-publishing came around once more to readily embrace the new digital formats; likewise, market cynics and critics as well worried—not entirely without grounds—that this new venue would only offer another opportunity to once again lower the quality of the overall publishing landscape.

Nevertheless, e-books have changed the way people interact with books by allowing readers to experience books at lower price points without the concern of a printed book they may not want to keep and therefore enticed people to try titles they would've normally passed over.

Ten years ago the publishing world of today would sound like something that fell out of another dimension. In a way it has, because technologies in existence today were not viable or viably presented in earlier times. There's still a great debate as to the future of bookstores. It's deeply troubling for anyone who values the written word to see so many bookstores vanishing from the brick and mortar world. Not long ago every mall housed at least two or three bookstores in addition to the wide array of local and large chain bookstores. There's certainly a valid case to make that the e-book phenomenon and online retailing has led to the decline of many of these stores, much in the way that music downloads destroyed old-style record stores and caused the near disappearance of music sections, even in large electronic retail chains.

Nevertheless, there are forces at work in the marketplace that indicate not everything is as it might appear. Despite the boon in self-publishing, there's been speculation as to the sustainability of such explosive publishing numbers in the years to come. This is due to a number of factors, not the least of which may be the simple reality that many authors who were only interested—or capable—of creating a single book have worked through the publication process and have since bowed out of the market. It may also be that some who haven't published have been turned away by horror stories of those who were published and were subsequently overwhelmed by the marketing gradient faced by new authors. Either way, the sustainability speculation is by no means an indicator that self-publishing is going away, but only that it too must adapt to a changing market.

The same can be said for e-books. The rapid evolution of available titles and capabilities of e-readers has led them to evolve into comprehensive entertainment platforms offering movies, music, and games in addition to books. There's a healthy dose of irony in this development, as the very devices that were created to foster book sales now offer intrinsic competition to books. Perhaps it's this glut of options, or perhaps readers are making a return to the traditional printed book, but there's still only a marginal portion of the reading market interested in purely electronic books. The majority of individuals who read still seem to favor the printed form.

The preferences of book media may have to do with the types of books people read. For those titles that people read once and never read again, the electronic book is an ideal option. On the other hand, to some the idea of books sinking to the level of "disposable" media, destined for one look and then deletion, is depressing. Even so, over time the prevalence of e-books may be influenced by environmental concerns. Printed books require paper, paper comes from trees, and the messy industrial process to manufacture paper is open to a debate exceeding the scope of this discussion. Nevertheless, true book lovers often cite the tactile experience of holding a book and turning actual pages as a timeless, serene escape from the electronic babble of modern society.

There's one underlying reality to be distilled from all these viewpoints: the way in which the publishing industry interacts with its readers continues to change and will do so for a number of years. Authors have the responsibility to at least be conscious of shifts in the publishing world in order to stay viable within the marketplace. As with everything else in the pursuit of publication, it requires research and diligence.

Now, with all that in mind, it's time to make an important decision. Segue!

The big question: self-, small, or large publisher?

With all the options available in the world of books, where and how one chooses to publish may best be handled with a pragmatic examination of each publisher level.

Before entering upon this discussion, however, it can be very useful for an author to consider his or her publishing ambition. For those who are interested in working with a single book, there may be an inclination to move toward self-publishing for its ease of entry and flexibility. For those who foresee several titles in their publication future, it may be better to go with a traditional publisher of any scale to establish a publishing relationship. This may be particularly advantageous for a starting author unable to secure agent representation or lacking economic resource for upfront editorial and book production expenses. Small publishers often prefer certain styles and genres, and can provide a more personal experience for authors they publish. Even so, relationships can be both mercurial and difficult to generalize.

So, let's take a look at the considerations of different publishing options.

Large publishers

The chances of landing a large publisher with a first book are quite remote, particularly so without an agent. As a general rule, large publishers won't look at manuscripts lacking agent representation. The traditional publication path still relies on agents vetting authors and their books. Under this model publishers are in the position to consider manuscripts that have some level of refinement and at least an agent's conviction of commercial appeal. Particularly for authors unknown to publishers, this path remains virtually unchanged. Considering as well that a publishing contract with a large publisher can be quite complex, it's perhaps best that an author have an agent as an experienced negotiator familiar with the customary, realistic terms of the business.

Also, unless an author already has some experience with marketing and promotion, it might be advantageous in the long run to opt for a smaller publishing outlet—self- or small—to tackle the learning curve of marketing. Even with large publishers, the reality of the publishing world today is that authors are expected to take the lead on marketing their books. Only the top A-list authors will have publisher assets out front on marketing efforts. Without any experience in marketing, an author might end up in the prickly position of having the muscle of a large publisher while lacking the individual marketing insight to make the most of that muscle.

One of the classic appeals of large publishers is the concept of the author advance. In the old days, part of the idea of an author advance was to help buoy the author economically until the book was published and sales revenue manifested. In the early 1990s the average advance hovered somewhere around $30,000. With all the changes in the publishing world and the market pressure on even large publishers, this number has dropped to a few thousand dollars for an unknown author. Additionally, in today's world authors are also expected to utilize this payment to fund marketing efforts.

The monetary value of an advance can vary dramatically. Author recognition, prior sales success, publisher confidence in sales, market trends, and agent savvy all have marked impacts on the advance. No matter the size of the advance, though, it's important for authors to remember that advances are typically made against expected sales of a book. So, while the advance is a guaranteed payment, no other monies will be paid to the author until book sales effectively earn back the advance. A book that fails to earn back its advance will not bode well for the author's financial standing with the publisher. In contrast, a book that exceeds sales estimates may profit the author in future negotiations.

Nevertheless, there are still decided advantages with large publishers. Top-notch editorial review, cover design, and practically unlimited retail distribution form some of the technical advantages. Large publishers also vary their publication interests through the use of imprints. This allows the parent publisher to specialize resources under subdivisions with specific genre interests such as science fiction.

On the subjective side, listing titles from a large publisher can add to an author's credibility. On the marketing side, while marketing expenses may be shifted toward the author, there's still a decided advantage for those authors with a large publisher behind them. Some of the elite reviewing services only review an ARC (Advance Review/Release Copy) several months before a projected publication date, a practice well within the realm of large publishers. In addition some of the elite reviewing services limit their independent reviews to titles from large publishers while exacting steep fees for titles from self- or small publishers. This is perhaps the most troublesome market bias that still lingers against those who are self- or small published.

Small and self-publishers: what makes them similar

For several years mentioning small and self-publishers in the same sentence could start a full brawl and end up with police in riot gear. All joking aside though, trends in the marketing world have left small and self-publishers with many of the same considerations.

In either case the responsibility of marketing falls entirely on the shoulders of the author. While this may be a cause to despair for some, it should be viewed as an opportunity to learn. There are many subtleties to acquiring professional reviews for books, for dealing with book award entries, and for an author's personal presentation to the wider reading world. Very few authors enter the publishing world understanding these subtleties; indeed, even some of the most experienced authors will attest that these are never-ending learning processes.

The advantage of being with a small or self-publisher is that the author will have the chance to make a few stumbles without committing a possibly unrecoverable error. It can also provide the author with vital experience so that when the time may come to deal with a large publisher and/or a major experience of popularity, the author has some understanding of the options and opportunities such moments present. The light of attention is indeed fleeting, and nothing can be more disheartening than to have a moment in the spotlight and squander its potential.

In terms of professional reviews and award competitions, self- and small publishers are now treated almost the same. There are some contests that offer dedicated categories for self-publishers, but for all purposes, the major delineation stands between large publishers and, well, everyone else. Professional reviewers no longer reject self-published titles outright; on the other hand, there are some reviewing services that have turned the table and will only accept self-published titles. Consider it the rise of the underdog. In either case the old preconceptions that once drew stark barriers between self-published and small publisher books have, for the most part, disappeared.

Small and self-publishers: what makes them different

Commonalities aside, there is yet a distinct divergence in the business model of small and self-publishers.

Perhaps the most significant difference is the publication cost associated with these respective options. Small publishers still follow the old model in which publishers absorb the production cost of the book to the point of publication. At that point the royalty rate is a reflection of the publisher's attempt to make a return on its investment in the book. Reputable small publishers will employ editorial service as part of book production, as well as cover design and internal layout, at no cost to the author. In effect, there's zero cost to the author to see the book through to publication.

The model is different with self-publishers. The royalty rates of self-published books are sometimes double that of small publishers because there is much less production investment on the part of the self-publisher. Instead, the costs of these services are deferred to the author, with the level of service denoted on increasing levels of attention and corresponding cost. Typically, self-publishers offer a narrow set of publishing templates that include stock cover art and internal layout at nominal cost to the author. More complex and perhaps professional options come with higher author costs. There are quality self-published books indistinguishable from productions by small and even large publishers, but this level of quality comes at considerable cost to the author.

In rough terms, an author can expect to front in the neighborhood of a thousand dollars or more to produce a self-published book, with a realistic cost close to two thousand dollars for a high-end, quality product. Most of this expense will come in the form of editorial service. Since this is the greatest cost center of self-publication, it's unfortunately the first place inexperienced authors will look to save money. There can be no bigger mistake. Poor editorial practices are the greatest single contributor to the bias against self-published titles and continue to dog some self-published titles to this day.

The counter balance to the up-front cost of self-publishing is the benefit on the back end. Royalty rates are much higher since production costs were offset to the author on a fee-for-service basis, thereby freeing the publisher from those financial impacts. Some self-publishers also allow authors more freedom to move their titles to other publishers, clearing authors from binding publishing contracts.

How large publishers leverage books to win in the marketplace

EVEN THOUGH LARGE PUBLISHERS OFTEN expect authors to take the lead on marketing, large publishers still have a monumental capacity that sets them apart: they can leverage the book market to, hopefully, produce winners.

How a large publisher markets a book will of course depend on the projected commercial success of the title in question. This may sound painfully obvious and simplistic, but such is not the case. Top A-list authors benefit from marketing expenditures large publishers reserve for their elite status. They have proven themselves commercially successful and so can constitute much more reliable sales figures for the publisher. This in turn allows the publisher to gauge major marketing costs within a projected revenue budget from book sales. Considering that a full page ad in a mass-run print magazine can cost upward of $150,000, and even short television commercials can cost tens of thousands to produce and purchase air time, these are costs that fall in the realm of corporate expenses.

While A-list authors have earned their publishers' marketing help through their commercial success, there's also the unknown author—or more often the "celebrity author"—who can also benefit from this level of marketing investment. How does this happen, if such authors have no prior publishing sales record?

The answer is simple for celebrity authors: their celebrity status gives them name recognition that can spur sales. For the unknown author, he or she will have to benefit from that rare moment of good fortune in which the book in question sets a publisher ablaze with sales expectations. In either case the publisher will put its marketing muscle to work.

The market leveraging can begin as early as the announcement of a publication deal with the author. Before a word is written, there's already media exposure to generate interest in the title. Weeks, perhaps months, before the publication date, the book can be released as an ARC for elite reviewing services to list and review. Marketing hype will continue to ramp up toward publication, at which point the author may be made available for media venues with high numbers of viewers. National advertisement will spread, not only from media outlets, but also within bookstores themselves, and premium electronic ad space will also be considered.

The idea is no different than any other marketing approach, and that is to create enough public momentum for social factors to drive book sales. The more people who read a book and talk about it will trigger even more people to read the book. If enough people read the book, it can become a cultural trend and drive sales further.

Yes, this is every author's dream. It should be noted, however, that not all of these campaigns work. In fact there's an irony within the world of large publishers. While as businesses they bemoan the decline in book sales, at the same time they've exhibited a tendency to offer lavish advances and expensive marketing efforts to leverage certain titles in the hopes of quick or trendy sales that capitalize on name recognition. These expectations sometimes fall far short of realization and leave the publisher with a large financial loss. This is the fate of some celebrity authors, and it has also been the fate of some books by political or news figures.

Despite these occasional disappointments, they nevertheless illustrate a key point that sets large publishers in a class by themselves. If they so choose, they're positioned to affect a tidal force on the book-buying market.

Book economics: price points, expenses, and royalties

REGARDLESS OF THE NATURE OF a book's publisher, one thing remains the same: once an author publishes a book, the author's publication aspirations now constitute a business. In Part 1 of this primer, I touched upon the tax consideration of incorporation to help cushion costs and shelter income at a lower tax rate. See the section "Economic and expense considerations." While such an option is certainly one to consider, even without exercising this option, an author needs to be mindful of the dollars and cents involved in book economics.

In Part 5, Regarding Marketing, I'll discuss the concept of author branding and books as products from a marketing perspective. For now simply consider a book as a product. Like any other product it will have an associated cost, a profit margin, and a competitive price range.

A good starting point to consider is the initial author expense for a book publication. Authors who find their way to a large publisher will have incurred minimal expense, their primary costs having involved the effort to secure an agent. In this route the largest expense authors might bear are independent editorial charges before submitting to agents.

With small publishers the publisher absorbs book production and editorial costs while the author takes the burden of marketing expenses, costs of reviews, costs of any award entries, and all postal expenses. Depending on the number of reviews, awards, and marketing efforts, it would be wise for an author to set aside several hundred dollars.

For those who self-publish, consider anywhere between $1,000-$2,000 for book production costs and an additional several hundred dollars in reserve for initial reviews, awards, and marketing.

Now, with those expenses in mind, it's time to look at post-publication economics.

Price ranges for books are of course influenced by the format of the book. In this section all references to price points will be to books without special formatting needs or heavy reliance on photos and images. Children's books in particular, because of their singular dependence on color art, live within a very different pricing regimen. Hardcover books as well reside within a different cost relationship due to their inherent production expense.

So before going any farther in this discussion, let's take a neutral stance and define a book as a straightforward work of text, physically manifesting as a soft cover, standard perfect bound, in the 100,000-120,000 word count range, roughly translating to 250-300 pages, depending on font, pitch, and internal page layout.

Price points for books can be a heated topic, as it constitutes one of the sticking points between traditional and self-publishers. Whereas traditional publishers will make the business decision of a book's price, some self-publishers allow authors the flexibility to set their own price points, within certain boundaries. Amazon's CreateSpace publication programs are notable for this flexibility.

Pricing for books will of course vary depending on their format. For electronic formats, such as Kindle and Nook electronic books, the "sweet spot" is between $2.00 to $2.99. Going below this threshold may create some skepticism as to the book's credibility or quality and leaves very little room for sale price incentives. Going over this price range is trickier territory. While more prominent authors have the name recognition to draw readers into higher price ranges, even they are often motivated to stick within the sweet spot to be competitive in a cost bracket that has been set by consumer interest as much as by market dynamics. Prominent authors also have the advantage of large, dedicated reader bases so that lower book prices can be offset by sheer sales volume.

The farther one exceeds the upper range of the electronic format sweet spot, the harder it may be to secure sales. Keep in mind that readers are sensible enough to understand that without the physical production of a book, the price point of an electronic book should be considerably less than the printed copy. This expectation may not always be realistic, but it's quite real. Pricing an electronic format as an increasing percentage of the printed book effectively eliminates the electronic book as a credible sales option for many readers. From an author's marketing perspective, one of the most enticing facets of electronic books is the prospect of luring a reader for a nominal price. It's a simple matter of financial risk assessment. Someone who may not be interested in a book for $16.00 may well be willing to give it a shot at $2.99.

With printed books the matter of price points may be more complicated. Several factors go into the price point of a printed book. After the initial cost to manufacture the book, there follows the various "cuts." For generalized numbers on a print book from a sales outlet, consider the following breakdown. The book's list price will typically be twice the manufacturing cost, so that 50% of the sale goes to recoup the material print, and 50% remains to be divided among the interested parties. Of that 50%, the retailer will typically take half, leaving the final 50%, or 25% of the original retail cost, to be divided between the publisher and author.

This is where the author's royalty rate comes into the equation. Among small publishers, for example, an author royalty rate runs around 40%, which means for a book that costs $8 to print, generating a retail price of $16, $8 will be left to be divided among business interests. The retailer takes half, or $4, leaving $4 for the publisher and author to divide. If the author gets a 40% royalty split, the author receives $1.60 from the print sale.

These numbers can of course vary widely, depending on the publishing route through which the book appears. With a large publisher the author's royalty share is lower, but there is the offset of sales volume. With a self-publisher the split is higher in the author's favor, typically in the 70% range, almost doubling the author's take in the above example.

Purchasing author copies from self- and small publishers will also run into varying costs. For the standard book referenced above, the actual printing cost will run approximately $6; with an end cost closer to $8, including shipping, sales tax, etc. This will be the cost to the self-published author. On the other hand, the author with a small publisher will effectively "cover" the publisher's expected royalty share on the book, thus inflating the author cost to over $9, including shipping, sales tax, etc.

The cost of author copies is an important consideration for consignment deals. A book consignment occurs when the author and a bookstore deal directly in stocking the book, rather than the retailer ordering copies from a distributor. Consignment deals work on percentage cuts on the *total* agreed sale price of the book, which can make things difficult for the author. Consignment deals typically run around the 50/50 range, basically an even split of the sales cost for the retailer and author. While taking home half the sales price sounds great, this has to be taken in light of the author's cost in providing the books to the retailer.

Reciting the numbers from the above example on royalties, let's assume it costs the author $8 to order author copies for personal stock. This stock is then handed over to the retailer for sale. If the original retail price of $16 is used, the 50/50 split provides the retailer with $8 and the author with $8, minus the $8 of the book's cost, providing a final profit of—that's right—$0. For authors to see profit from consignment sales, the retail price of the book needs to be raised. The $16 retail would have to be inflated to $18 for the author to see a profit of $1 (50/50 of $18 leaves $9 for the author, minus $8 print cost, leaving $1).

So, while consignment deals aren't very appealing in terms of book pricing, they do offer the opportunity for authors to have their books displayed in local bookstores. Welcome to the world of author compromises. This extra sales channel can offset the author's added task of maintaining stock at the store, assuming the books sell. This is an important assumption, for authors need to be wary of consignment deals that also include a monthly shelf or stock fee to carry the book. This will be one more cost that has to be figured into the book's price point so that the books don't sell at a loss.

Independent book signings offer authors the greatest flexibility in pricing. These are events outside consignment arrangements or bookstore stocking, such as an author appearance at a local fair or author-arranged book presentation. In such a setting the author has only the print expense of the book to consider. So for the retail book at $16 that costs the author $8, the author can offer a 25% discount, sell the book at $12, and go home with a profit of $4 on each sale. One caveat is that some events incur a table expense to support the event that needs to be factored at the end of the day into net profitability.

When all is said and done, the considerations boil down to a few simple points. With a major publisher the author will have virtually no say in the pricing of a book. With small publishers the author may have some flexibility but will most likely see the most return from individually sold copies at appearances. With self-publishers the author will have greater price control and perhaps lower print costs, allowing more flexibility on both consignment and individual sales.

By now it shouldn't be a mystery that the profit returns are low. A common joke among authors is that no one becomes an author for the money. Nevertheless, every author still dreams of reaching the pantheon of profitability. All expenses should be weighed against the hard returns of sales. If an author will only see one to two dollars of return for each book sold—print or electronic—any promotional expenditure can be recalculated into a book sales number to return the cost. This is not to say that some costs are investments for long-term exposure and author credentialing, but more to say that it's crucial to keep an eye on the bottom line before incurring unrecoverable expenses.

So now that we've talked about some of the nuts and bolts of the book business, let's take a look at some of the nuts and bolts of books themselves.

Considerations for book design

WHETHER CHOOSING A SMALL OR self-publisher, the importance of good design practice cannot be under emphasized. In either of these publishing segments, it's wise to peruse other titles the publisher has produced. Scrutinize the quality of the cover art, examine the back cover for proper layout to entice a reader, and most definitely sample the text for its quality.

This may sound like nitpicking, but this is the exact process a reader employs in selecting a book for purchase. Book design itself is a profession that large publishers take very seriously, and so dedicate a corresponding investment to ensure success. Small publishers may lack these resources; self-publishers will charge for professional-grade services. In fortunate cases the author and publisher will collaborate to produce what their combined experience and wisdom judge as a compelling design solution. In unfortunate outcomes an author and/or publisher will generate a cover design from stock templates and open source, generic images. This can be a kiss of death for a book.

Keep in mind that readers don't know at first glance whether a book is from a large publisher, small publisher, or self-publisher *if* the cover design is properly executed. Sit in any bookstore and watch readers browse books. Better yet, consider your own practice of evaluating a book for purchase. Almost all potential readers will give a book something I like to call the "three-count exam."

The three-count book exam

First: A glance at the cover—most marketing professionals claim a reader judges a book by its cover in as little as three seconds. Common wisdom may say not to judge a book by its cover, but the reality is that this is exactly what happens with potential readers. While a reader's interest in a cover is entirely subjective, there are cover design philosophies that work with visual perceptions to grab interest. These include text placement, use of color palettes, positional relationship between cover elements, and text contrast. Text should *always* stand out on the cover.

Second: Cover looks interesting? Hmm. Let's flip this book over and take a look at the back. Is the summation interesting? Is there a captivating catch-line to spur interest? Is there some kind of outside critical praise quoted for the author or title?

Third: Back cover was indeed interesting. Let's take a look at the text. Most readers will look at the book's opening lines, flip through pages and randomly read a few more lines on each flip, and may even take a peek at one of the last pages.

✸

SOUNDS GOOD; BUT THERE'S AN obvious question: what about potential readers who peruse online, not in a physical bookstore? Interestingly enough, there's little difference. The first look—the visual capture of a cover—can occur on a search list. The idea that the first view of a cover might be a thumbnail-sized image is yet another concern for cover design-ing. The second look occurs when a potential reader clicks on the book link and proceeds to the book product page. The back cover matter—the catch-line, praise quote(s), and author and title information—typically appear at the top of a product page. Last but not least, the third look occurs when a reader clicks on an excerpt, utilizes a Look Inside feature, or reads the more detailed book synopsis and review sections.

When everything is said and done, remember that the book is your product. Just as cheap-looking merchandise reflects negatively on both the product's quality and the manufacturer, a cheap-looking book reflects poorly on the author. Notice that there's no mention of the publisher here—publishers don't have their name on the cover of a book, but the author does, so it's the author at risk of a negative impression. Likewise, consider this question: have you ever heard someone say they turned away from a book purchase because they didn't recognize the *publisher*?

The quality of a book *product* will always be a concern for an author. Large publishers diminish this concern by virtue of their resources and established expertise. Small and self-publishers may be questionable in this key area, so it's critical for an author to ensure that the book, as an end product, is market worthy.

Considerations for book length

IN THE WORLD OF SHORT stories, length is a key factor in determining market option availability. The longer the story, the shorter the list of potential markets, and the harder it may be to see the story through to publication. Even the difference of a thousand words, between 5,000 and 6,000, can have a huge impact. A story at 5,000 words still has the main market segment open; a story at 6,000 words, on the other hand, will see only a fraction of the market segment open. This might not seem to be a relevant concern in the book world, but word count is still an important consideration for beginning authors.

The simple truth of the book marketplace is that all traditional publishers—and most literary agents—won't entertain the notion of a lengthy book from an unknown or fledgling author. Keep in mind that the longer the book, the bigger the editorial investment on all sides, from author to agent to publisher. For agents and publishers there are the added concerns of marketability for longer books and the business inclination to take longer books and revise their framework so they can be separated into two or even three serial titles. To inexperienced authors this may sound like creative sacrilege, but this is where market awareness comes into play. There's a strong market *and* reader interest in stories that span three or more individual books.

The book series has become a powerful presence within the book world, and it makes sense on several levels. First and simplest of all is that readers are often intimidated by the time demand of hulking books. Just like digesting an overflowing plate of food compared to smaller dishes with parceled servings, it's easier for readers to digest the idea of experimenting with a shorter book and then moving on to later installments within the series. Second, a series allows authors, agents, and publishers to benefit from multiple sales across the titles that comprise a series. Separate titles within a book series are mutually supportive in terms of sales and in this regard everyone wins. Third, a *completed* book series holds the potential of a multi-book deal that will once again entice agents and publishers with an investment that provides future returns.

Which circles back to the original question: what is a marketable book length? For fledgling authors, or for those seeking their first book publication, anywhere between 90,000 and 110,000 words is a reasonable length. Going over 120,000 is a risky proposition; many small publishers and quite a few agents will shy away from books past this point and may not even consider books going past 150,000. This can seem discriminatory to inexperienced authors when they see established authors publishing mammoth tomes in the range of seven hundred or more pages, but the keyword in this observation is *established*. There's a general trend among publishers, particularly the larger publishers, to allow authors with proven sales success to expand the length of their titles.

A caution to keep in mind is that some large tomes receive an unwelcome criticism from readers and critics alike, and that is "word bloat." Depth is a wonderful thing, but creative over-indulgence is another.

New or fledgling authors won't have an established sales base to justify a lengthy book. In fact, authors who insist on pursuing lengthy books will be met with suggestions to edit the book down to a marketable length or expand it into a series. In most cases it's advice well worth taking. For those rare few who create a lengthy book that can't be curtailed or separated into a series, perhaps the most accessible option will be to pursue self-publication.

Self-publication of a lengthy title will involve some unexpected expense considerations. Remember that editorial costs are commonly calculated on a per-page basis, so longer manuscripts drive up those costs. A longer book will also increase the book's production cost—also calculated on a per-page basis—forcing the author to either raise the book's end price or cut profit margin to maintain a competitive sales point. Neither option is particularly attractive because both limit the book's profitability.

It's easy for an author to "get lost" in the depth of a book and end up with word bloat, particularly when first experimenting with book writing. Experience with short stories can be extremely beneficial in alleviating this problem. Short stories require strict word discipline; by their very nature *short* stories demand authors to put sharp consideration into every word and phrase of the narrative. For many authors starting their first book, 100,000 words has the deceptive appearance of an endless creative margin.

General writing experience will be an author's best guide. The more you write, the better you will be in judging how much word space you'll need to convey the characters and story in question.

Distribution acronyms: ISBN, ASIN, UPC, EAN and LCCN

Print books don't follow a direct path from their publishers to a store's physical or virtual shelves. Books are procured by wholesalers from publishers and then in turn moved along to retail outlets such as bookstores and libraries. This process is managed through the use of different numeric codes, the acronyms of which are often tossed around with little explanation. The principal players in this alphabet soup are the ISBN, ASIN, UPC, EAN and LCCN. Each has its place in the process of a book's distribution to the greater reading world.

Books printed by traditional publishers—small to large—will have these number assignments managed by the publisher during the publication process. With self-published titles the various assignments may require additional up-front fees from the author before the publisher will process the applications.

ISBN

Part of the overall book distribution system relies on a numeric code known as the ISBN, or *International Standard Book Number.* Any book in a retail store will have an ISBN; it's the number over the barcode on the lower right corner of a book's back cover and is denoted with the prefix ISBN. The ISBN was originally limited to ten digits; after 2007 the standard was expanded to thirteen for international compatibility. This is why books are often listed with both ten and thirteen digit numbers.

In simple terms the ISBN is a unique numeric assignment to identify and track a book for ordering purposes. Since the ISBN for a book is specific to the book's edition and publisher, it's a powerful search tool for outlets. Because they are unique, the ISBN can delineate between a first or second edition, a hardcover versus paperback, or a print from publisher A versus publisher B. This specificity is why community book sites such as Goodreads rely on ISBN searches to match a particular version of a book with a reader's review experience. It allows people to connect with one particular incarnation of a book, regardless of when it was released or which publishing company was responsible for the release.

Likewise, a book without an ISBN is not searchable and therefore will not be available for distribution and search through the Big Three distributors—Ingram, Baker & Taylor, and Bowker—utilized by book-stores, including online stores such as Amazon. Aside from understanding that these three organizations are the principal players in print distri-bution, the mechanics of their exact function work behind the scenes of the publishing world and transcend the scope of this discussion. Suffice it to say that if a book has any hope for wider commercial distribution, it must be part of the catalog housed by the Big Three, and therefore must possess an ISBN.

During a book's pre-publication production, the publisher can register the book with an ISBN and its identifying search data, also known as *metadata*. The key point to remember is that the absence of an ISBN code can hinder a book's market potential. Depending on the type of book, there may be instances where this isn't a concern, such as a trade publication with a narrow reading base. Books without an ISBN will only be available by sale direct from the publisher or author.

For those who self-publish, ISBN assignment is often listed as an option in a production package. There will be more on production pack-ages in the next section. Unless a book happens to fall within a special set of circumstances where potential distribution through bookstores and libraries is *not* important, it behooves the author to secure an ISBN. For authors who choose to be extra industrious by forming their own publisher imprint, ISBN codes can be purchased in blocks for assignment to future publications. This will be discussed in the last section of this part, "A bigger picture: have your own publishing imprint." In cases where a book will appear in different countries or in different languages, each of these geographic- or language-specific editions will require its own unique ISBN.

ASIN

As opposed to the ISBN, the ASIN is the *Amazon Standard Identification Number*. This number, assigned by Amazon, is used to track products within Amazon's inventory. For print books the ASIN is the same as the ten-digit ISBN. For non-print books, such as Kindle e-books, Amazon assigns a unique ASIN.

UPC and EAN

The UPC, or *Universal Product Code*, is a twelve digit number set appearing under the barcode of items for purposes of retail tracking in the United States. In contrast, the EAN, or *European Article Number*, is composed of either twelve digits—European standard—or thirteen digits—U.S. standard. The EAN number is used in place of the UPC for items sold in Europe and most of the world outside the United States.

When it comes to the world of books, however, the delineation is not as clear. While the United States uses the UPC standard, within the United States the publishing world foregoes the UPC in favor of the EAN. A numeric prefix is added to the EAN—978, or in some cases 979—to produce the thirteen number ISBN discussed above. The EAN prefix is referred to as the *Bookland* designator because it transcends the traditional geographic distinctions of the UPC and EAN.

EAN-5

The EAN-5 is the smaller barcode appearing to the right of the larger ISBN barcode on the back of a book. For an ISBN barcode to be scanned in the United States it must have the accompanying EAN-5 number. Together, the thirteen-digit ISBN barcode and the EAN-5 are referred to as the *Bookland EAN*.

The purpose of the EAN-5 is to encode the price of the book and its currency. For example, U.S. dollars are designated '5' before the price of the book. So, if a book sells for $16.99, the EAN-5 code would be '51699'.

There are two exceptions within the EAN-5 code system. First and most common is an unspecified price code of *90000*, used by self-publishers to allow authors to individually set their price points with various retailers. This blank code will not automatically scan a set price, but will instead refer to a price entered in the local retailer's proprietary database. If an author makes an agreement with a bookstore to sell a book for $16, the store enters this amount in its registers and ties it to the book's ISBN.

The second exception, and much less common, is when a book price transcends four digits, that is, the cost of the book exceeds $99.99. This is a specialized realm of high market books such as photo collections or university texts. In this case the 90000 code can be used with the actual price entered in the local retailer's database as described above.

LCCN

The LCCN, or *Library of Congress Control Number*, is yet another numeric assignment for book tracking. It differs from the ISBN in two important ways. First, only libraries will reference this code. Second, whereas an ISBN is unique to each edition of a book, the LCCN applies to the creative content itself, independent of editions or formats. An LCCN makes a book available for libraries across the United States and serves as a tool for librarians to search a book's bibliographic information via the LCCN. It's important to remember that the LCCN is *not* a copyright on the content.

✦

FOR FINAL CLARIFICATION, THESE NUMBERS appear in different parts of a print book. The LCCN appears only on the inside data page of the book, along with the ISBN, publisher, copyright holder and copyright year, author, and assorted credits. The back cover of the book will bear the Bookland code—the EAN, also known as ISBN-13, plus the EAN-5 price designation code.

Of late there has been an increasing debate over the necessity of obtaining an ISBN. In the realm of large and most small publishers, books automatically receive ISBN codes. Self-published titles, on the other hand, may not. The debate centers on the issue of bookstore stocking of a particular title. Realistically, it's true that bookstores are unlikely to stock books from unknown or fledgling authors; however, without an ISBN the book won't be available for stocking from the Big Three distributors should it gain sales momentum and thereby bookstore interest. Self-publishers often refer to access of the Big Three as *extended distribution*. While some opinions figure this a distant consideration, it may be wise to look at ISBN assignment as an investment in the future. Whether an author purchases ISBN codes independently or pays a self-publisher for assignment, the cost is minimal in comparison to overall potential expenses.

It boils down to a single question: would you forego a potential sales outlet? Looking back only a few years ago, this very same discussion involved the option for e-book format. Negative opinions figured e-books as a fringe fad, whereas positive opinions considered them a viable sales alternative. From today's perspective, an opinion arguing against e-book availability would sound ludicrous. Also, the dream of anyone who markets a product—and yes, your book is your product—is to reach a state of passive sales, that is, sales that don't require direct marketing intervention. Without an ISBN and the distribution opportunity it offers, passive sales can be difficult to achieve.

Book production services

The popularity of self-publishing has helped foster the option of book production services. *Book production* involves the nuts-and-bolts process of turning a book from its generic word processor format into a book format; in short, all the steps required to make a document file into the recognizable form of a book, cover and all, in either print or e-book.

Authors who work with small or larger publishers will find production services included at no cost in the process of seeing a book through to publication. The publisher fronts the associated expense and then recoups any costs through royalty share.

Self-publishers follow a different model in which the production costs are factored into various publication packages fronted by the prospective author. Conversely, authors now have the option of using independent services to procure these essentials before interacting with a publisher. Independent book production services will manage all of a book's technical aspects up to but not including the actual publication, though they may help interface the author with a publisher.

Self-publisher production packages consist of levels entailing more extensive—and expensive—options for editing, book templates, fonts, interior layouts, cover designs and, for books containing graphics or photography, various levels of graphic integration. On the business side, the package levels will entail book listing with distribution services, ISBN assignment, copyright, complimentary author copies, and perhaps the option for hard cover and/or e-books. In essence, the more options, the more cost for the package.

Various self-publishers have sought to build their reputation in the publishing world by the quality and personalization of their services in the book production process. On the other side there are self-publishers who offer authors an option direct to publication, bypassing costs of editorial services. Amazon's CreateSpace is notable for offering a model with stripped down publication paths. For minimal expense, publication can be achieved without enlisting editorial and layout expenses, with the understanding that the quality of the book is the author's responsibility.

This is where independent book production services come into the equation. While reputable self-publishers offer editorial guidance on book design and layout—again, everything that gives the book its appearance outside of the actual text—authors will find that their options are limited to those included in the selected production package. For those using Amazon's CreateSpace, it will fall upon the author to make many decisions on the final appearance of the book. Independent production services can guide authors who want to make these decisions outside of a publisher while ensuring a professional, attractive presentation of the book. As a matter of reference, I have utilized the editorial and design services of Stories to Tell Books, most notably for the book you currently hold in your hands.

Whether or not to use independent book production services is an author's discretion. One distinct advantage is that the author will be purchasing a cover and book design outside of a publisher, so that if the book transitions to a different publisher, there's no need to alter the cover. Remember that the book's cover is a vital recognition tool. While independent services are not free, they may offer editorial and design interaction with an editor on a more personal level than one might experience with a publisher. Publishers want their authors' books to succeed, but an independent editor can be a valuable asset—and ally—in an author's career outside of a publisher's specific domain.

Even if an author chooses not to utilize a book production service for the purpose of taking a book to self-publication, there's always the option of using editorial services to refine a manuscript prior to submission for agents and publishers. No matter how good an editorial eye an author might possess, there's no substitute for an impartial, professional editorial review.

A word on audiobooks

AN INCREASINGLY POPULAR OPTION FOR authors is to have their written works converted to audio format for *reading on the go*. While Amazon's Audible can be considered the most prominent player in this part of the market, there are numerous potential sales outlets for audiobooks themselves. The best known of these outlets are through Apple and its various devices and, of course, Amazon. As a result, audiobooks represent a sales channel authors shouldn't overlook. This section will offer a quick glimpse of this opportunity.

Despite the surge of audiobook sales in recent years, the market can still be considered a relatively new place. Yes, audiobooks have existed for quite some time as books on tape or books on CD, but the emergence of digital audiobook files available for download bears some similarity to the early days of the e-book market. Some books are well suited for this type of reader experience, while others perhaps not so. Just as with e-books, there's certainly a convenience factor. However, people who are dedicated readers want to experience a book in their own reading voice, at their own pace, free of outside visual distraction, rather than have a book presented to them in the cadence and vocal emphasis of another person.

The path a book might follow to manifest as an audiobook has much to do with the book's publisher. Large publishers, and a number of small publishers, will take on the process of audio conversion as part of their relationship with an author. For self-publishers or those who publish on their own, the path to audio conversion may involve extra service cost from the self-publisher or the responsibility falling on the author to secure the conversion.

Either way, the basic process of audio conversion involves a narrator reading an author's work. Depending on the length of the written work, this process will likely entail hours of studio time. A basic, single narrator recording will cost hundreds of dollars and can quite easily transcend a thousand dollars. For more fanciful productions involving multiple voice actors, sound effects, or even musical pieces, the production cost can quickly escalate. If an author happens to contact a narrator and the author is comfortable with the narrator's reading style, there may be an opportunity to curtail some of the expense.

Another option is for authors to do the narration themselves. In general, unless an author has some type of vocal and production experience, it's probably best for an author not to read his or her own work. Just as it's ill advised for authors to independently edit their written word, it can be ill advised for authors to handle production of their own audio recording. Narrating a book is only one ingredient of the process. Achieving proper audio quality requires specific sound equipment and the proper software to edit the completed recording.

How the cost for the audio conversion is recouped varies with the contractual agreement between the narrator/recording service and the author/publisher. The simplest is an up-front payment. For authors funding the conversion, this capitol expense might surpass their budgets. Another option is the royalty share, such as the 50/50 model used by Audible's recording service, ACX. As a one-stop audiobook producer, ACX provides authors, publishers, agents, and narrators a marketplace to pitch titles and services. Once the respective parties link their interests, they can make an agreement on conversion cost and method of payment.

There are other options for audiobooks outside of Audible and ACX for those who may want a more hands-on approach. Price, service, and support will vary, but as with all things related to the publishing world, be cautious of low-cost productions. Just as with print and e-books, a poorly produced audiobook will be a difficult sell.

No matter the path chosen, authors need to understand that an audiobook production is one more contractual agreement involving their books. For authors with traditional publishers or for authors purchasing audiobook production through a self-publisher, this legal component of the process will likely be handled for the author. For authors independently approaching audiobook conversion, it's important to understand the specific copyright language involved in the recording agreement. As with everything else, read the fine print.

Literary agents: some pros and cons

IN THE PAST UNDER THE old traditional model of large publishers, acquiring representation from a literary agent was often considered a requirement for an author to break into the major publishing market. Indeed, in today's world, with the amount of published authors to choose from, large publishers typically don't take unsolicited submissions. Instead they watch the market and see which authors are meeting with success before reaching out to those authors. Other than this, an author's interaction with a large publisher is still initiated by a literary agent.

For those who have rejected the old publishing model as extinct, the issue of whether or not to get an agent will most likely depend on the measure of an author's success. At a certain point the amount of non-writing tasks the author must manage, along with the size and complexity of possible opportunities, can be too much for one person to handle. The expertise, market knowledge, and familiarity with deal negotiations that an agent brings to the table can be indispensable. For those authors comfortable negotiating on their own *and* confident in their understanding of contract language, they may choose to pass on an agent and keep the associated commission cost in pocket.

The most likely path between an author and an agent will occur when the author has written a first book or has published to the point where the author is looking to step up in the marketplace. In the various sections preceding this discussion, the pros and cons of large publishers have been discussed, yet the fact remains that for many authors the best chance at financial success rests with landing a contract at a large publisher.

These considerations aside, there are several factors to keep in mind when looking for agent representation. In some cases these concerns are no different than the preparatory steps one would follow in submitting a manuscript to a publisher.

Almost to a rule, agents will not entertain incomplete fiction manuscripts. In this regard the non-fiction market is completely different wherein a query will often outline a book proposal to the agent, along with the author's credentials, so that the proposal can in turn be pitched to a publisher. If the publisher takes the proposal, the author then moves on to complete the book. Conversely, fiction books have no value until completed. Certainly, this is the view of agents and publishers. While there are agent deals for multi-book contracts to fiction authors who are yet to write those books, those deals form a minority of what occurs and represent a distinguished sector of publishing deals. For the starting author the book must be completed.

A manuscript should already be edited. Agents are not in the business of teaching authors grammar or doing basic editorial tasks. A poorly worded or edited query letter, or most certainly an excerpt with poor grammar and spelling errors, can guarantee a quick rejection. Suggestions will most likely be made on higher editorial levels, such as advising the author to expand a part or character or trim down a section that slows the narrative flow. Once the agent moves to shop the manuscript to publishers, it will be a clean manuscript. This, of course, doesn't exclude the publisher from asking for additional revisions.

As with publishers, it's imperative to research an agent's stated interests. Agents gain their expertise in certain segments of the market and achieve sales success through established professional relationships with editors at large publishers. While there are aspects of publisher negotiations that are common throughout the marketplace, the particular trends or technicalities of a certain genre or sub-genre will require an agent with a stated interest in that particular area and thereby the associated publisher contacts. The Internet allows agents to host their own websites so that authors can see what genres of books an agency represents and perhaps the current member agents who work with various genres. Submissions to agencies with such specialties should be addressed to the corresponding agent.

Business concerns after agent acquisition spark the debate over agent necessity. A common misconception among inexperienced authors is to believe that once an agent is secured, a lucrative publication deal is soon to follow. The stark truth is that securing an agent holds no guarantee that a book will be published. In fact, in today's publishing world, securing an agent won't even guarantee that a book deal will be struck with a large publisher. For those who discount the need for an agent, they cite this very possibility. Why share royalties with an agent when the book lands with a publisher the author could've approached on his or her own?

In addition, smaller publishers often use standardized, non-negotiable contracts. There are even some small publishers who state outright that they won't interact with agents at all. In these cases the need for an agent is dubious at best.

On the other hand only an agent can guide a manuscript into the prospective hands of large publishers. Agents still hold the keys to the doors of opportunity in this segment of the market by the very nature of their market expertise and relationships with editors. In a real way an agent can be thought of as an author's representative to the "insider's club" of the higher publishing market. Agents will use their market knowledge to court publishers amenable to an author's book and possibly to an author's greater career interests.

Agents are publishing-industry professionals. As such they have ethical guidelines to which they should abide and to which the author should be familiar to distinguish reputable agents from the questionable. The principal stamp of propriety among agents is membership in the AAR, the Association of Authors' Representatives. Their full canon of ethics for member agents is available at their website, aaronline.org. In addition to the reference material and agencies listed with AAR, virtually every major genre of fiction has a principal membership group—Science Fiction Writers of America, Mystery Writers of America, etc.—that will provide genre-specific agent recommendations along with their own tips and guides for courting agents.

First and foremost, as a rule, agents and agencies should not charge authors for services. The agent model works on commission. Through this model both the agent and agency have vested interests in the success of the manuscript to earn their royalty share. Agency costs are mitigated by the commission, which should run 10-15% on domestic sales and perhaps up to 20% on foreign sales. The higher rate is due to the use of a subsidiary agent for the foreign market.

It's the author's responsibility to research a prospective agent. There are numerous informal websites where authors exchange experiences with agents; however, like any other type of "user" reviews, many of these need to be taken with a large grain of salt. Disgruntled authors, like disgruntled product reviewers, often don't admit if they followed an agent's submission requirements, if a manuscript was properly edited, or if the agent in question was in fact interested in the manuscript's genre. Use common sense when reading such reviews. As with any good user review, look for those who mention specifics about interaction with the agent.

Agents, as with publishers, deal with an excess of authors. The boon of self-publishing has inspired more people toward publication than in the past and so increased the demand on agents. Unfortunately, while quantity has gone up, the question of quality remains open. Agents, like publishers, now have the luxury of watching the small and self-publishing world to see which authors are meeting with success in sales, awards, or both. This somewhat Darwinian process allows the higher levels of the industry let the marketplace do the vetting process.

After all, everyone likes a proven commodity. As a publicist once told me, the world would much rather build on momentum than try to create momentum.

Preparing a book submission/query package

NOW THAT WE'VE GONE OVER the basic concerns and considerations before seeking publication, it's time to look at what needs to be done to secure publication.

For those who decide to go with a self-publisher, the path will be simple. A publisher will be chosen, a publication package selected, payment made, and then the publisher will provide specific instructions as to the book production process. Sometime later a published book comes out the door.

For those who wish to go with a more traditional approach—whether through first seeking agent representation or directly securing a publisher—a book submission package will have to be assembled. Authors who cut their teeth in the short story marketplace will find this a familiar process, while for authors jumping straight into book publishing it may take some work to get everything together.

Let's take a look at the ingredients in a submission package.

Cover/query letter

First item is the cover or query letter. Although submission instructions vary between targets, the query letter is still a common standard. As with a cover letter for short story submissions, the letter should be grammatically clean and concise in message.

Authors often bristle at agents' reliance on query letters. Authors feel it's unfair to pitch a book of 100,000 words in a letter of perhaps a few hundred words. What this perception fails to understand is that agents are piled with submissions, and the query is the only practical way for agents to get an immediate grasp of a submission. Like it or not, authors must understand that courting an agent is in many ways no different than how the agent will attempt to court a publisher, and the book will attempt to court readers. If an author can't effectively pitch a book in a letter, it's unlikely the book will attract publisher or reader interest.

The first paragraph of a query should contain the basics, such as book title, word count, genre, and prospective audience. Never describe your book as a title for *everyone*; the "fun for all ages" claim is a clear signal that you haven't researched your audience. *Every* book has a defined market segment: adult nonfiction, women's mainstream fiction, literary fiction, Gothic horror, cozy mystery, etc. You know best what you wrote. If you're unsure where your book fits, do some physical or virtual book browsing to find similar titles and then see their genre listing.

There's a fine balance in the wording of a cover letter. It should be enticing while not crossing the border into ad copy. The opening paragraph containing the book's data is objective. The next paragraph, containing a short description of the book, can have more flash; this is the paragraph to entice an agent or publisher. The remainder of the letter can be used to objectively sell yourself as an author by citing important prior credentials and any bio information supporting the genre of your book.

Synopsis

In terms of presenting your book, the synopsis can have as great or greater an impact than an excerpt. While an excerpt provides a snapshot of your actual writing, it's the synopsis that allows an agent or publisher the chance to judge the overall structure of a book. Specifically, the goal of the synopsis is to render in factual detail the basic elements of character, plot/theme, and resolution.

Not all targets require a synopsis. On the other hand, those targets that do ask for a synopsis can ask for either a short or long—full—synopsis. The current trend is toward the short synopsis due to the fact that agents want to evaluate a submission as fast as possible. If a target asks for a *brief* synopsis, this typically means a paragraph or two. Such a synopsis can be included in the cover letter in lieu of the regular three or four sentence book description.

If the idea of writing a synopsis makes your blood run cold, welcome to the club. There's hardly an author out there who doesn't groan at the prospect of writing a synopsis. Besides the nerve wracking question of whether or not the synopsis reflects your book in a way that appeals to an agent, there's the basic writer's concern: you wrote a *book* because you had a book length idea, and now it has to be condensed to a few paragraphs. Don't despair. There are many blogs and advice columns online with excellent tips on common do's and don'ts. The Writer's Digest website is a good place to start.

There are two tones a synopsis can embody. The common demand is for a dry, factual rendering of the book wherein the book excerpt becomes the designated forum for the author to exhibit specific writing qualities. The far less common demand is a more flashy condensation of the book that allows the author to show some writing chops. The best way to discern what tone an agent or publisher prefers is to check their respective websites for submission instructions. At some point while discussing a synopsis, there will be tag lines such as "describe your book in detail"—factual synopsis—or "show us something we haven't seen before"—consider breaking out the flash. It may be worth the time to write a separate synopsis in each tone so that you have both ready to go when needed.

Agents' websites often list examples of successful queries and synopses to clarify the desired tone of submissions. If examples of such queries and synopses are made available, it's well worth the time to study them and read the accompanying agent notes.

A short synopsis likely runs in the neighborhood of a page or so, although the idea of a "page" is somewhat subjective when dealing with email, due to the absence of page breaks. Think of writing a short synopsis in the same way you would write an essay—yes, just like high school. The first paragraph should make a strong, compelling statement as to the book's narrative arc and the placement of the main character(s). The second paragraph can explore the overall plot and how it relates to the main character(s). In closing, the last paragraph should summarize how the plot concludes and, just as importantly, its impact on the main character(s).

Remember that a synopsis is a dry rendering of the book. Statements should be blunt, concise, and lack any dramatic description. For example, if a pivotal moment in a book describes a big action sequence in which one character kills another, keep it short and sweet: *After a car chase John kills Bill.* Do *not* embellish: *After a thrilling car chase that keeps readers on the edge of their seat and inspires relentless page-turning, John finally gets the upper hand on Bill and gives him his due justice.*

In contrast a full synopsis can cover several pages. This allows more discussion of characters and plot elements, although it's important not to get lost in what may be considered minor detours within the plot. As with the short synopsis, be sure to close with a firm statement of plot conclusion and character catharsis.

At this point it should come as no surprise that there are format standards for a synopsis:

1. Contact information, upper left of first page, with each piece of information on its own line.
2. Title, skip a line, the word SYNOPSIS, all capitals, centered beneath contact information.
3. In the header, denote the book title, the word *Synopsis*, and a page number.
4. A synopsis is always written in third person, present tense, regardless of the narrative perspective, and verb tense of the book.
5. Body paragraphs. For a short, one page synopsis, it's acceptable to single-space lines within a paragraph. For a longer synopsis, stick with conventional double space.

6. The synopsis is not a strict blow-by-blow rendition of the plot; the short synopsis describes general plot and theme directions, while a full synopsis has the space to follow pivotal plot segments.

7. All major characters, entities, and places should be typed in all capitals the first time they're mentioned.

Excerpt

The last part of a submission package will be the book excerpt. Like the synopsis, not all targets will request an excerpt; indeed, there are quite a few agents who only accept a query letter. While this shouldn't be a reason not to query a particular agent, the advantage of submitting to agents who do accept an excerpt is self-evident.

Targets that request an excerpt will generally specify what part of the book they want to see. As a general rule the excerpt will be from the beginning of the book, as this is the most sensitive aspect of the book for hooking a reader. The most common excerpt requests will be the first few pages, the first chapter or thirty pages, or the first three chapters. Regardless of the length of the excerpt, it should go without saying that these pages need to be the most carefully scrutinized and edited pages of your book.

In some cases agents won't specify which pages of a book to send as an excerpt. While it may be tempting to send the *best* pages of the book rather than a specific part of the book, keep in mind that pages from within the book will be read out of context, thereby deflating their dramatic impact. Likewise, there are some who recommend disregarding agent specification and sending a full three-chapter excerpt, the argument being that the agent will ignore material that wasn't requested. In contrast there are agents who claim they automatically dispose of submissions that fail to adhere to their instructions.

An often-cited tip/gripe from agents, and one that I feel is well worth mentioning as general writing advice, is to understand the importance of a book's opening. The last thing agents want to hear, or the author complaint that serves to annoy agents, is that the book really gets rolling on, say, page fifty. The agent response to this, and the point authors should consider, is that the book should then *start* on page fifty. This is the main reason agents most often request an excerpt from the beginning of a book. Remember that immediacy is a key element in the structure of a narrative to hook a reader, and it should never be forgotten that agents are first and foremost professional readers.

❄

Once all the ingredients are assembled, it's time to submit. Postal submissions will be straightforward in their packaging in that you print the required materials. As with short stories, *never* send your postal query with a return receipt. Never fold multi-page submissions; always send them flat in a yellow envelope adequate for the volume of pages. Electronic submissions can vary in process; some agents have a query submission system in place of email to avoid spam while others will use email instructions. Be mindful of these instructions. Specifically, be sure when to paste all materials in an email and when to add them as attachments. Some agents use spam filters that auto-delete any email with attachments.

With everything on its way, sit back and start preparing the next query package. Most agents and publishers don't ask for exclusive submissions, so you can make the most of your wait time by sending out rolling batches of queries. In general three to four queries at a time are a safe recommendation. As with short stories, you don't want to send out a large batch of queries only to later realize you overlooked a mistake or improvement.

The book is published—now what?

As an author it's a labor of love to write a book. The exacting process of revision and self edits comes next, followed by the no less exacting process of locating and submitting to publishers. Whether self-, small, or large publisher, once the publisher is secured and the contract signed, there follows the production process of professional editorial review, book design, and—at long last—the joy of publication.

Far too many first-time authors live under the illusion that publication is the end of the book process rather than one early step. With all the hundreds of thousands of titles published each year in the United States alone, how many of these are actually noticed by readers? Sadly, the majority of authors rapidly succumb to marketing fatigue after their books are published. We'll take a look at marketing specifics in Part 5, Regarding Marketing, but for now suffice it to say that there are some preliminary steps to take in building credibility for yourself and your book.

To illustrate these points I'll share my personal post-publication experience from my first book, *Remnant*. I've said in several interviews that I was under the gross misconception that, given the sheer number of books sold every year, any book would surely possess some default, built-in sales figure. After all, the pipe dream presented to the greater public is that money just appears on the doorstep once an author publishes a book. Reality couldn't be more different. For me, I discovered that a book's default sales figure is zero. After saturating my personal "friends and family" sales circle in the first few weeks following publication, my sales dried up. The quality of my book wasn't the issue; the problem was that nobody knew about my book.

Once a book is published, the real work begins: marketing, marketing, and more marketing. For everyone enjoying the accomplishment and satisfaction of seeing a book through to publication, they will find themselves amid a competitive marketplace, vying to grab the attention of readers. Fortunately, while there are many books, there are also many readers—far more readers than books in fact. The challenge is to get your book in front of them.

I'll take this moment to relay another learning experience from my first book signing. I went to the *LA Times* Book Festival to do an author event coordinated through AuthorsDen, with high hopes that I could move a good number of copies. When I arrived at the festival, I realized just how small a fish I was in the very large ocean known as the publishing world. There I was, a first-time author with one book, competing for attention among A-list names and many other authors with established publishing records and established marketing efforts. The lesson that hit me over the head was not only the importance, but also the absolute necessity, of marketing my book.

Rarely does a first-time author enter the post-publication phase with a clear grasp of the marketing world. As the saying goes, it's one thing to know and another thing to do. Without digressing into specific marketing topics, let's say for now that every book comes out on equal footing to the marketplace. Marketing efforts make the difference between what's noticed and what will languish. Marketing can be daunting to learn. Likewise, at times the effort invested, coupled to sometimes dubious returns, can make the effort seem both discouraging and a towering impossibility.

There's no spoonful of sugar to wash down the occasionally bitter pill of confronting a vast publishing market with one small voice. Too many take the size of this challenge and use it as justification to do nothing, allowing the daunting process to foster resignation. However, if you do nothing, your book—your labor of love—will be lost in the crowd.

Considerations for book reviews: a first step after publication

Garnering book reviews is part of a sound marketing strategy and an important process for launching a book. If the book's publisher offers an ARC, reviews can be in place to help build buzz for the book's publication. Without this benefit, start coordinating reviews the moment the book is published.

Before going out for reviews, be sure to understand review content. The art of critique is a very human process, so reviews will consist of both subjective and objective content.

Although these two perspectives live in their own realms, they will inevitably overlap. A book can be engaging, but if it has technical deficiencies, these problems will detract from the subjective enjoyment of the book. Conversely, a book might be a work of technical perfection but lack an engaging plot. Depending on the reviewer, the separation between the objective critique and the subjective critique can be stark or non-existent. Professional, market-level reviewers are notable for their ability to concentrate on the objective qualities of a book before taking them in context toward subjective critique. Readers who do informal book reviews will be more prone to let their subjective critique of the book displace or overwhelm their objective response.

Well-written reviews offer coveted *tag* or quote lines. These are the commonly seen blurbs plastered on the jackets of books. The accepted fair use of any review is that the author can excerpt quotes from the review and even link them with ellipses to condense a statement, so long as the quotes or condensed statements do not alter or mislead the reader from the statement's original intent. When quoting, always remember to cite the source of the review. The source can be equally if not more important than the quote itself. A quote without a source is not only invalid but can also blemish the author's credibility.

Reviews come in many flavors, and each has its place. In my opinion and experience, market-level reviews are a great aid in building an author's confidence and for learning what narrative qualities translate through one's writing. They can also be the best source for promotional quotes, as experienced reviewers are aware of the commercial aspect of their critiques.

For purposes of this discussion, let's break down the categories of reviews into peer reviews, casual reader reviews, and market-level reviews.

Peer reviews

Critiques of this nature, particularly if the reviewing author is a known name, can be a great boost to a fledgling author's work. However, access to known authors can be difficult to attain. Keep in mind that if you approach a known author to ask for a review, the author in question may be receiving numerous requests for reviews. Known authors, like any other author, work within time constraints. As much as a given author may love to read, committing to a review is a different matter.

Before enlisting another author to review a book, it's prudent to look at other reviews said author has written. As with any other form of written expression, there are well-written reviews and poorly written reviews. Remember, once the author posts a review for a book, it's difficult to have that review retracted. If the author has reservations about reviewing the book, for matters of professional courtesy the reviewing author should perhaps decline to review or have a private discussion with the author of the book in question. On the other hand, if research shows the reviewing author can be harsh, perhaps it's best to reconsider the review request.

A sticking point that can arise with author peer reviews is the *review swap*, where two authors agree to review each other's book. Again, familiarity is important before engaging in such an arrangement. There are plenty of stories of authors who enter these agreements only to receive reviews lacking substance or perhaps no review at all.

A brief Internet search will even reveal sites that run exchanges for author reviews. Whether or not to engage in this practice should be taken with a respectful dose of caution. Personally, I avoid swaps. Even among fellow authors with whom I am friendly, I don't promise a review nor ask for one in return. My feeling is the same as it is for any other reader: if the author likes the book enough to be compelled to write a review, that's great. If my book does not sufficiently engage them to compel a review, then I respect their opinion. I would never ask a fellow author to write a review to which he or she isn't honestly committed.

Nevertheless, a great quote from a recognized author lends critical validity to a book. Remember that quotes are like good investments in that they don't diminish over time.

Casual reviews

Casual reviews from readers can be great for developing a *man-on-the-street* appeal, but they are of questionable use when attempting to develop critical validity for a book.

In today's world there's the unfortunate reality that some readers review books without having read them. The most direct evidence is when reviewers post several reviews a day for books. Obviously, there's a time issue in these cases. This disreputable practice can be detected in reviews by a few tip-offs: the review is short—not just a capsule review, but no more than a few scant words—the review lacks any specific references to events or characters in the book, and last but not least the majority of the review's content is paraphrased from the book's back cover blurb. Be wary of services that offer to wrangle dozens of reader reviews for posting on Amazon or Barnes & Noble. A little research will reveal that some of these reviewers exhibit the disreputable tip-offs cited above.

In another area, it's natural for authors to ask friends, relatives, and acquaintances to write a reader review. While it may be great for one of these readers to give your book a kind review, it's not good practice to cite compliments from reviewers who are part of an author's personal life, for reasons of potential bias.

As a final note on casual reviews, remember that the main objective with reviews is to earn promotional quotes. Casual readers are not necessarily talented at promotional writing or, in particular, at writing a review. The author must be careful in moderating grammar or spelling errors when quoting so as not to be suspected of altering the review. A positive review is always a wonderful thing, but if it can't be quoted properly, or the source citation is from an odd user handle from Amazon, the review won't be of practical marketing use. By "odd user handle", I mean the following: would you be more inclined to trust a review quote from someone named "John Smith," or from someone who goes by "crackerpaste66"?

Market-level reviews

Market-level reviews are professional critiques from book reviewing services, blogs, and print periodicals, with the delineation between them often bridged by presence on multiple media outlets.

Before submitting for such a review, be sure to research the service and follow the submission instructions. These are outlined on the service's website, as well as what genres are eligible for review, and any restrictions they might impose on submitted material. For example some services will only review an ARC; others will only review particular genres such as science fiction or romance. While failure to follow a service's instructions may not result in a loss of payment, it will most likely involve the loss of the physical book submitted. All reviewing services will either retain submitted books or donate them to charities promoting literacy.

Market-level reviews offer a number of options that translate beyond the review itself and shed some light on the reviewing process.

Any legitimate reviewing service should offer a free avenue for reviews and should not operate solely on a fee-based model. The free avenue will come with two important caveats: one, there's no guarantee a book will be reviewed at all; two, if the book is picked up for a review, there will be no stated time frame in which the review will post. Some review services will only hold submitted titles for a certain time period, stating to submitting authors that if the review doesn't post within that period the book will be passed.

For books that are reviewed, the review should always come with a disclaimer that there's no guarantee of a positive review and that the book will be judged on its merit. Some reviewing services even offer an opt-out such that if the book receives a negative review, the author can elect not to have the review posted. In these cases the author may be offered advertisement space in lieu of the review.

Of obvious importance is to examine the fee structure for paid reviews. Due to evolving market dynamics, reviewing services need to generate revenue from their reviews to stay in business. Part of that revenue stream is derived from services coordinated with a review. The first item on this menu will be an offer for a paid expedition of the review—the service guarantees your book will be reviewed within a time window from receipt. This is a great asset if you want to coordinate several reviews or events. If a publisher does not offer an ARC for pre-publication review, then an expedited review is the best method to collect critical feedback and promotional quotes within the first weeks after publication.

The second item on review services is to bundle some type of promotional service with the review. These vary in character but often include premium placement of the review within the service's publication outlet—Internet, print, blog, or combination—bundling a review with a text, podcast, or radio interview, inclusion of a press release, and last but not least an advertisement with the service's publication outlet(s).

Regardless of the source of your book's review, before submitting, look at the character and content of the service's reviews. Remember, writing a review is itself an art form. A well-written review should discuss more than a book's plot and whether or not the reviewer "liked" the book. In addition it should discuss in some length the flavor of the author's prose, the quality of character development, the refinement of the narrative, and the impression these create. While these parameters may not seem particularly relevant to a book, keep in mind that as an author you want to receive accolades for both the book and you the author.

A good market review will tout both these aspects. Remember that while readers buy books, they are also very loyal to the authors of books they like. A book, as a product, is a singular entity, but you, as the author, constitute the brand of future titles. You want a review to help build a return customer base. This thinking enters the realm of marketing, but for now keep in mind that as an author you want to share stories, and the only way to do that is to have readers take interest, not only in a particular tale you wrote, but in the *way* you wrote the tale. That involves building a reputation for your narrative voice, the unique imprint on your writing that marks it as something only you could write, that is recognizable as yours and yours alone.

Though market reviews can constitute an expense, market-level reviews are investments that pay endless dividends. Market reviews have the significant advantage of their name recognition as the source citation of review quotes. I found the review services I use by looking at quotable sources in books from large publishers.

Promotional quotes can see exposure beyond the book jacket of their respective title. A common practice in the publishing world is to include reputable quotes for an author's previous titles in the first few pages of a current title. Not only do these help substantiate the author's credibility, they are essentially free marketing for past titles. In addition, if you work with a publisher that doesn't offer an ARC for pre-publication reviews, display past review quotes that discuss general writing quality on the current book cover. Depending on the publisher, quotes for the current title can be substituted as they become available.

Another bonus of market reviews is a *review tear sheet*. This is a professionally prepared document of the review with the letterhead of the reviewing service. The tear sheet is a handy tool to include when preparing marketing material for a book.

Not all market-level reviews will independently post their reviews on Amazon. There was an odd disagreement between Amazon and reviewing services a few years ago wherein Amazon purged all market reviews. The claim from Amazon was that the services' fees violated Amazon's user-review policy of *honest, unpaid* reviews. The reviewing services countered that payments were for expedition, not content, but Amazon refused to budge. The glaring inconsistency in Amazon's claims was that, while Amazon purged reviews from reputable services, at the same time Amazon did nothing to police the reviews of serial reviewers, that is, individuals who post bogus reviews for ten or twenty books per day as part of paid-review recruitment scams, as discussed earlier under *Casual Reviews*. Amazon's stance was made more curious by allowing authors to utilize their Author Central page to individually cite review quotes from market-level reviewing services. More on this in Part 5, Regarding Marketing.

The end result of this mess was that some market-level services no longer post reviews on Amazon, or they instruct their reviewers to post their reviews under their own names with no mention of the service. Either way, as an author you can still utilize promotional quotes from the review via your Author Central page.

Here are some reputable reviewing services:

- *Feathered Quill Book Reviews* (www.featheredquill.com)
- *Readers' Favorite* (www.readersfavorite.com)
- *Bestsellersworld* (www.bestsellersworld.com)
- *Pacific Book Review* (www.pacificbookreview.com)
- *Reader Views* (www.readerviews.com)
- *San Francisco Book Review* (www.sanfranciscobookreview.com)
- *Foreword Reviews* (www.forewordreviews.com)
- *Kirkus Reviews* (www.kirkusreviews.com)

Both Foreword Reviews and Kirkus Reviews are premium book review sites. They are known to be very tough on their reviews, so a good review from these sites is all the more notable. However, their reputation comes at a steep price. Expect to pay several hundred dollars for a single review, whereas the other reviewing services here will offer expedited reviews typically in the one hundred dollar range.

✸

As a final word on reviews of any source, authors need to understand how best to handle criticism. Sooner or later there will be a review that doesn't exactly light the birthday candles. It's difficult to swallow negative comments in a review, but authors can learn from these comments. If a review offers legitimate objective critique on the structure or technical aspects of a book, it's well worth the author's time to consider those comments.

On the other hand, subjective negativity in a review can be much harder to process. These comments can be divided into two categories: one, the more palatable statement that the book simply wasn't to a reviewer's tastes; and two, the much harder to accept "attack" review. The former should be taken in stride; the latter should be ignored. The Internet is a wonderful forum for negative people to rant and rave to their heart's content, often for no other reason than to spew their vitriol. An author should *never* engage with a "hater" or "troll" in a war of words regarding a review. It makes the author look petty and unprofessional and only ramps up the level of attack. There have been a few glaring examples of how disastrous these exchanges can be for authors.

Negativity aside, if a review posts in a forum where an author can reply, such as a blog, the author should consider at the least to thank the reviewer by focusing on the positive aspects of the review. Even a reviewer who complimented the structure of a book, but didn't enjoy the particular subject matter, can be thanked for being objective. The only time an author should correct a reviewer is if the review contains a glaring or misleading factual error, and even in these cases it should be done as diplomatically as possible. The last thing an author needs, particularly a fledgling author, is to be labeled as a difficult person. It's a sure turn-off to both readers and reviewers.

Be brave—enter an award contest!

GLOWING REVIEW QUOTES ARE A great way to bolster a book's appeal, but nothing serves better to grab a potential reader's gaze than an award seal. The visual impact alone of an award seal can have a dramatic influence on a reader's first impression. It's not a guaranteed way to sell a book, yet it serves an undeniable benefit if it earns the book a second look from a potential reader. For greater promotional purposes it also adds the tag *award-winning author* to one's name.

Some of the reviewing services open to authors whose books appear through self- and small publishers also sponsor book award contests. With that said, it should come as no surprise that the world of book awards shares some similarities to the world of book reviews. Book awards, however, are an all-or-nothing proposition. While even a lukewarm review might offer a quote usable for promotions, when it comes to book awards, either a book will place or it will not. Although this prospect can be a deterrent when considering the cost of entry fees, a book award is similar to a market-level review in that it serves as a promotional tool throughout one's writing career. Award contests are a more risky investment than an expedited review, yet the increased risk can offer increased reward.

Reputable award contests follow the same basic formula. Eligibility instructions will detail any restrictions on the type of publication, the publication date, and genres. The contest will be broken down into submission categories, which may be numerous. A submission form will require information on the author, the book, the publisher, a list of entry categories, instructions on the total entry fee, and the number of copies to be submitted. Expect to send one or two copies—print or e-book, depending on principal publication format and category—for a single contest category and one additional copy for each extra category. Contests hosted by review services may offer a discounted review for books the service has not yet critiqued. If this bundle option is offered, it's an economic bonus worth considering.

In an ideal world the planning for book awards should start well before a book is published. All contests run on rolling periods of publication dates, thereby limiting title eligibility within a year or two after the publication date. After this time period the contests available are few and far between.

Be mindful as well of entry dates in relation to entry fees. Most contests will open their submission period a year ahead of the award announcement and encourage early submission with reduced fees. For some contests, such as the Independent Publisher Awards (IPPYs), this discount is significant enough to cover the cost of a submission copy and postage.

Once again, research is key when scouting suitable award contests. Fortunately, the contests supported by reputable reviewing services, such as the ones referenced in the preceding section, are also reputable. In being reputable, they carry merit. The stark reality is that while there are many award competitions available for authors, there are those that carry little recognition outside their local supporters. This isn't meant to diminish the judging criteria or prestige, but for the investment of book copies and entrance fees required to enter award contests, it may serve better economic sense to try a larger, more established contest.

So how does one delineate between contests?

There are several basic criteria to follow when researching contests. The most obvious thing is to make sure the contest in question has a category that fits well with your book. There are some contests that claim to judge books of any genre in one lump category, and that's a red flag. Established contests, even contests that are genre specific, will have a detailed list of categories in which to enter. Not only does this ensure your book is competing against titles of similar flavor, but in the event you receive award placement, the award category serves as an immediate label to your book's character.

A book on display will have to draw some attention to get a potential reader to view the back, flip through the pages, and get a feel for where the book sits in the literary landscape. Having a label on the cover announcing award placement in a category not only draws attention but also informs the reader of recognition within the book's genre. This holds true as well for cover images at online book sites where an included award graphic can catch the gaze of a perusing reader.

When looking at contests, get a feel for the contest's history. Use the Internet to search out winners of prior years. A contest with several years of history not only ensures that the contest will come to a conclusion but can testify to the caliber of competition. While it's nice to recognize the names of winning authors, perhaps of greater interest is to see the publishers of the books that placed in award rankings. Cadres of unknown publishers, or publishers that only have a handful of published titles, suggest the competition may be a fringe event with very limited scope.

Established contests also issue press releases for prior contest announcements, often detailing the volume of entrants they received. This too will help gauge the level of competition, the comparative prestige of award placement, and the scale of the contest. When it comes to contests, a rising tide lifts all boats. If a contest has a large pool of entrants, then exposure and prestige will also be greater for those who receive award placement.

Contest fees are an inseparable part of the process. Reputable contests are significant undertakings that involve many hours of work from preliminary readers and judges. Time can translate to large labor costs for the contest host. A review of contest rules will often show that most reputable contests have more than one reader assigned to judge each book, particularly in the latter rounds of the contest. While it's tempting to correlate the size of a contest and its entry fees, there is in fact no valid correlation. The typical contest entry fee will run anywhere between $75 and $100, often with discounts for additional category entries.

Category entries are a key component when planning award contest economics. Some books clearly reside in a specific genre. Other books, however, may span several genres. Anthologies in particular can be submitted for multiple entries due to the fact that contests often have separate categories for short story collections. The book in question can then be entered under the short story category, as well as whatever genre(s) it encompasses. While the ability to enter more than one category offers more opportunities for award placement, it can rapidly drive up entrance costs. If a book appears suitable for three different categories, the cost to enter a single contest can mushroom to the range of $300 after factoring in the cost of submission copies.

The best way to contain contest costs, and the best way to improve chances for award placement, is to be mindful of where a book best fits among the award categories. When in doubt, look at past winners within a particular category to see how well your book compares. If your book's content is a far departure from previous winners, it may be time to reconsider that award category or the contest itself.

After an award contest announces its winners, the host may offer publicity packages to the authors. Take time to consider these offers. They will often come at significant discounts to standard pricing and will add to the contest's default publicity of press releases and website announcements.

A useful strategy for planning award entries is to look at the critiques your title earned from various review services. If the book received a favorable review from a particular service, there may be a better chance of award placement in a contest sponsored by that service. There's no guarantee, but at least there's the confidence from one reviewer at the service finding value in the book.

After all is said and done, are contests worth the expense?

The obvious answer is that for the winners, yes, and for those who do not place, no. Indeed it can be both frustrating and expensive to invest in contest entries and walk away empty handed at the end. However, it's a worthwhile risk. Ask yourself one simple question. If you were offered two books, their covers concealed, with the only information that they are of the same genre and one book had placed in an award contest, which book would you choose? Readers will ask themselves the same question.

On a personal note, I can share my experiences on this matter. In 2012 I had the opportunity to visit the Miami Book Fair. It was an exciting time because I was down in Miami to collect my awards from the 2012 Readers' Favorite Book of the Year contest, and I had just found out the night before that I had collected another three awards from the 2012 USA Best Book Awards. So, not to be obnoxious, but more to gauge the value of having at that point seven national book awards, I mentioned my awards while talking with assorted publicists, editors, and publishers. I can't stress enough how the complexion of the conversation changed after mentioning the awards. Professional business tones immediately turned to wider eyes and direct, personal interest in my current books, future projects, and me as an author.

I've noticed a similar effect during author appearances. All my display materials include my awards, and when I get the chance to engage a prospective reader in a conversation, I always mention that my books have been recognized with multiple awards. This has to be done tactfully, of course, but the impact is noticeable. It doesn't guarantee a sale, but it certainly creates attention where it may not have existed.

As with any other effort to distinguish a book from the crowd, awards are about building objective credibility for the book and its author. It's not about bragging rights, but it most certainly is about setting your book apart. Remember, there are roughly a million titles published every year in the United States. Amazon alone is estimated to list several million titles on its website. Only a handful will ever be recognized with a single award, much less multiple awards. Do awards guarantee sales? No, but then nothing in the publication world is a sales guarantee. Building sales starts by building awareness, and awareness is built by setting a book apart from the crowd. Book awards are a definitive and lasting step in this essential process.

When researching award contests, be wary of those who condemn *all* contests as "vanity" awards. Due to the interconnected nature of the Internet, a handful of blog articles blasting award contests for the self- and small publishing worlds have had the opportunity to spread their poisonous roots. Certainly, there are disreputable award contests handing out placement to any title submitted; however, larger contests do not fall under this cloud.

Other criticisms—and issues worthy of research to deem a contest's validity—revolve around the collection of entry fees and the nature of award publicity. There's a definitive economic reality to entry fees. Although some of the most esteemed book awards in the nation are supported by various grants and donations, the situation is far different in the self- and small publishing worlds. As I described earlier, contests require significant investments of time, labor, and, therefore, cost, which many contest hosts simply cannot sustain without entry fees.

Tied in with the debate on entry fees is the matter of entry categories. Criticism here stems from the claim that multiple categories are created to increase opportunities for entry fee collection. There will always be an open question as to how many books compete for placement in any one category of a contest, although common sense will suggest that some rather obscure categories will indeed draw fewer entrants. Most contests cite a total figure of books entered, not a specific breakdown for each category. The biggest shares of entries, of course, go to the most common categories.

While a contest might abide by valid judging standards, there is the possibility that within a particular category there were only a handful of titles. At this point the value of an award may in fact be questionable if readers are left wondering how many other books there are to compare. Second placement in the broad category of Mystery Fiction can say more than first place in "Mystery, fiction, cozy, Southeast Region." For someone who's looking for a cozy fictional mystery set in South Carolina, that's great. For those outside that very pointed area of interest, such an award might not be of any service.

The same can be said for award publicity. While the top book awards receive support from donors and grants, they also receive publicity from these very same entities. These entities in turn have a vested interest and media capacity to gain attention for the award winners. In the worlds of self- and small publishing, contest hosts have publicity tools but most likely lack the media pull or resources of older, more established hosts. Just as authors who are self- or small published are looking to build their recognition, so too contests in this realm have to build their reputation to gain recognition.

In short be wary of small or unknown contests with high entry fees and a wide number of entry categories, for these may indeed fall under the dubious title of vanity contests. The general trend of contests is to expand as recognition grows hand in hand with a growing number of entrants.

A bigger picture: have your own publishing imprint

Within the realm of self-publishing, there exist two distinct options. The first and most common is for an author to employ a self-publishing company via a book publication package. The publisher executes a level of editing included with the package, coordinates book design, and the book goes to print. At this point the book will bear the self-publisher as the publisher of record. For those new to the publishing world, or for those who have a happy home with their self-publisher, this will remain the popular option.

On the other hand, a second, and perhaps more dynamic option, is for an author to create his or her own publishing imprint, take independent control of the editorial and book design process, and then secure publication. In effect, with this option, the author becomes the publisher and so retains complete control of the book in question.

So how do authors become their own publishers? It can be achieved in just a few steps.

1. Consolidate editorial and book design sourcing.
2. Acquire ISBN codes.
3. Establish imprint and publish.

Whether or not to act upon this option will involve several decisions. With a conventional self-publishing route, the publisher may still exert some control over the pricing of the book, and the book will bear the self-publisher's name as the publisher of record. The issue of pricing can be significant, whereas the publisher of record may be a more personal matter. For some authors there's still a desire not to be associated with known self-publishers out of concern for lingering bias within the publishing world. While an author imprint may be unrecognizable, it won't be recognized as a known self-publisher.

1. **Consolidating editorial and book design sourcing**

   These two vital steps, and an author's level of comfort in accepting their responsibility, will judge the comfort level of establishing an imprint. Services such as CreateSpace allow authors to choose their covers from stock images and templates or upload custom cover designs. Unless you understand the commercial intricacies of cover design, it's best to have someone familiar with cover work design a cover for you. The same can be said for editorial services. Again, as an example, CreateSpace offers increasing levels of editing; conversely, if you are comfortable with a particular book production service or an independent editor with whom you've developed a professional relationship—that is, someone who "gets" your writing and narrative voice—you may benefit from utilizing that person's expertise.

Why go this route? It may seem unnecessary extra effort, but there are other considerations to keep in mind. By following this route an author will effectively own the book, independent of any outside concerns. The cover design—the book's face identifying it to the reading world—can remain intact no matter what road the book follows over its publication life. Likewise, for those who want to keep all options open, by using an author imprint there are no obligations or restrictions from a publisher.

Remember that editorial and book design services are the two biggest parts of book production. If you're in a position where you're comfortable managing these on your own, or you have a trusted book production service on which to rely, then the only other hurdles to being your own publisher are to secure ISBN codes and choose a name for your imprint. In fact, by the time you've covered the steps of editing and book design, the book is ready to portal to any publisher since the book production is complete and in your hands.

2. **Acquire ISBN codes**

    Once the details of book production are ironed out, it's time to purchase some ISBN codes for extended book distribution. Although there are three book wholesalers for the United States—Bowker, Ingram, and Baker & Taylor—only Bowker is the official, registered seller of ISBN codes.

    Bowker has set up a convenient purchase page for ISBN codes, which can be found at www.myidentifiers.com. Pricing is skewed toward bulk purchases, with a single ISBN set at $125 and a bundle of ten at $295 as of 2015. There are larger bulk purchases available, but these are perhaps unrealistic options unless there are plans for publishing several existing novels. From this same website Bowker also allows purchase of barcode images for the back cover of book jackets. These barcodes facilitate potential bookstore interaction and sales via the title's Bookland identification—EAN, ISBN and EAN-5. See the earlier section *Distribution acronyms* for a refresher on these codes.

A quick Internet search will reveal numerous sites offering ISBN codes for far less than Bowker's prices—in some cases, ISBN codes will be advertised for only a few dollars. Even CreateSpace offers ISBN codes at a price discounted far below Bowker's rates. What, you might ask, is the catch? Only by purchasing from Bowker can you ensure universal compatibility of the ISBN and the right to use your own imprint. Those who discount ISBN codes do so by effectively reselling the ISBN to an author. These resellers buy ISBN codes in vast quantity and thereby receive deep discounts. They then place a profit margin atop an individual code and generate their "discounted" price. However, when the book goes to publication, the imprint will be the *reseller* because it's the entity to which the ISBN has been registered.

While some sites bury this important caveat in the legalese of end user agreements, CreateSpace is at least up front in their explanation of ISBN pricing and what avenue to follow to use your own imprint. On the other hand, there have been numerous reports that ISBN codes purchased from resellers have incompatibility issues with CreateSpace.

The long and short: be very careful if you choose to buy ISBN codes from a reseller. Bowker is the only *legal* source of original ISBN codes in the United States.

When purchasing ISBN codes, keep in mind that each *edition* of a book will require a unique ISBN. An edition is defined as a format, so if a book appears in hardcover, paperback, and e-book, it will consume three ISBN codes. Given that almost all books have at least a print edition and an e-book complement, the ten-code bundle from Bowker most likely makes the best economic sense.

3. **Establish imprint and publish**

    At this point in the process, you'll have a completed, edited book with a cover design and ISBN code(s) for print and/or e-book formats. It's time to find a publishing outlet.

    For many authors, the simplest solution will be to use CreateSpace for its accessibility and its ability to portal directly to Amazon. Opinions vary as to the commercial intentions of Amazon's presence in the market, but the fact remains that it is the retail heavyweight in the publishing world. A book that does not appear on Amazon foregoes a major retail outlet. On the other hand CreateSpace is far from the only option. Services such as Ingram Spark and Smashwords offer just as many—if not more—options.

    Publishing services other than CreateSpace and Amazon forego some of the advantages of being exclusive to Amazon by offering extended distribution and royalty opportunities outside of Amazon. These royalties are derived from sales between the Big Three distributors and other retail outlets. For those interested in e-book publishers, there are numerous options, many of which will also list with Amazon.

    Whichever path is chosen to realize actual publication, the steps follow the same basic format. As the author you will upload your manuscript, cover art—if created by an independent source—and ISBN code. Even though services like CreateSpace and Ingram Spark tout the ease of their processes, if an outside source such as a book production service was utilized for editing or cover art creation, such a service will most likely be able to coordinate the upload process as well. For those concerned about making a mistake, or for those uncomfortable with the technical requirements of certain file types—particularly for cover art—allowing a production service to handle the upload may be well worth the relatively minor expense for professional expertise.

    The turnaround from upload to publication can be very fast. CreateSpace often cites a window as short as two weeks; anecdotal evidence from fellow authors I've spoken with puts the time closer to four weeks. This will of course vary with any additional editorial services employed, but nevertheless, once a book is uploaded, it will be ready for the masses in little or no time.

One of the advantages of publishing in this manner is the ability to revisit a book already in publication. There will be a fee associated for any changes, but it's an option worth considering as a return investment on a book. If several good reviewer quotes, or even a few award placements, become available, a front page can be added with this promotional information. Award seals or quick brag quotes can be added to cover art. Perhaps of most interest, however, is the ability to go into the text itself to correct a problem that missed editorial review.

Summation: the book world in a nutshell

In the end, as with everything else in the publication world, how a book reaches publication is a matter of preferences and ambitions. Large publishers offer the most market muscle behind a book, but their doors are typically closed unless an agent can be secured to represent a book and its author. Small publishers have no up-front costs on book production but balance that savings against lower author royalties on the back end. Self-publishers offer greater royalties, and eliminate query hurdles of small publishers, but face the same marketing challenges as small publishers and involve up-front production costs. Authors who utilize their own publication imprint have perhaps the greatest creative and economic control of their work at the balance of additional costs and extra effort.

No matter the publication route chosen, remember to apply some basic market knowledge to the book itself. Book length is an important consideration, as well as the quality and nature of the book cover. Remember that a cover is the face a book presents to the reading world, regardless of format. Regarding formats, keep in mind options for audiobook conversion. And, of all other concerns, be sure the text is in the best editorial shape you can achieve.

All roads lead to marketing once a book steps out into the world. The foundation of this ongoing effort can be established through a few quotable, professional reviews and perhaps recognition in the world of book awards. From there will stem larger marketing concerns.

Now if there's an opportunity to segue, there it is—time for Part 5, Regarding Marketing.

PART 5:

Regarding Marketing

"Hey, I published a book. How about that! Now what happens?"

B ooks can be thought to exist in three parts: inspiration, creation, and perspiration. Inspiration involves the initial concept for a book, creation involves summoning that concept into written form, and the perspiration comes in marketing. Of these three processes, marketing never ends, as opposed to the very finite processes of inspiration and creation. Without marketing, the stark answer to a book's post-publication fate is that it will be forgotten.

To avoid that dismal doom, we'll take a look at the following topics.

- Marketing fundamentals, part one: author branding and author platform
- Marketing fundamentals, part two: media marketing materials
- Pundit recommendations: how to keep them in perspective
- Marketing realities of self-, small, and large publishers
- Make the most of what's free
- Virtual book tours and blog promotions
- Claim your own corner of cyberspace: build a website and/or blog
- Meet your audience: book signings and interviews
- The fine print on press releases
- Economic considerations for marketing
- To charge or not to charge: gifts and giveaways
- A simple, sample marketing plan
- Moving forward: be the proverbial rolling stone

If you gather a group of authors in a room, the conversation will always turn toward two hot topics: self-publishing versus traditional publishing and how to effectively market. Although these debates involve very decided opinions, they lack any definitive answers. Marketing is in some ways no different than what an author has to consider when selecting a publisher, in that any decision has pros and cons.

The goal of this part is to examine some of those pros and cons from a macroscopic view rather than break down specific marketing micro-processes. There are entire volumes written on each subject of marketing; nevertheless, it's important for an author to understand marketing fundamentals before venturing into the marketing world, even if that venture is made with the aid of marketing professionals.

Of those subjects perhaps the hottest is the use of social networking. This too is covered by a wide array of dedicated books, and likewise the effort here isn't to discuss or delineate specific social marketing plans but more so to discuss initial considerations before making those plans. Specific social marketing plans can be as mercurial as the world of social networks itself. That's no surprise, given the pace at which services rise, fall, or get assimilated by larger services.

In addition to objective considerations to marketing, there are also subjective considerations; specifically, intrinsic factors the author brings to the marketing effort. When marketing efforts are evaluated or discussed, it's the subjective factors that often make the difference between efforts that are productive and those that don't meet expectations. The secret to marketing—and it's not off the mark to think of it as a secret—is for an author to find a marketing effort that plays off one or more intrinsic strengths. Just as marketing outlets look to build on existing momentum, so too authors should perceive and capitalize any existing promotional qualities they possess.

Whereas publication can be a relatively straightforward discussion, marketing involves an author's background, an author's time availability, an author's financial resources, and an author's perseverance—all with no guarantee of sales success. Sales, however, are not the initial goal. The first goal of marketing is to build awareness. Readers must be made aware of an author's presence in the publishing world before they will buy books. How effectively awareness translates to sales is a question even professional marketers skirt with the utmost delicacy, no matter their confidence or bluster.

To have an honest discussion about marketing necessitates confronting some less-than-rosy realities. Although the next few paragraphs will sound pessimistic and unappealing, they provide crucial sensitivities for what awaits after publication.

In some ways marketing exposes the ugly underbelly of the publishing world. Marketing efforts can involve serious sums of money without any guarantee of returns. Whereas the old days of vanity publishers and their murky interaction with authors have been mostly eliminated from the landscape, the more open and forthright path of publishing has shifted some less-than-honest players to now call themselves publicists or marketers. It's unfortunate, given the majority of hard-working, dedicated, ethical professionals who want to help authors succeed. Nevertheless, the lack of guarantee on a marketing effort and some characteristics of the Internet have allowed questionable entities to ensnare authors.

Given the difficulties and uncertainties of marketing, marketing fatigue is perhaps the greatest source of author resignation and cynicism. It's easy for a new or fledgling author to succumb to negativity when confronted with the uphill battles of marketing. The summation often cited by fledgling authors is that large business interests within the publishing world have effectively locked up premium market segments through blatant cost barriers. The difference between backing from a large publisher and any other publisher can be stark indeed. For those outside the large publishers, there's no hiding that there's a definite pay-to-play system in the upper levels of the marketing and publishing world. To cite an example, just to *display* a book at one of the major book trade shows can cost hundreds of dollars, while to appear at such venues can easily cost over a thousand dollars.

There's even a tide of toxic cynicism claiming—not unfairly, in some aspects—that many business interests in the publishing world view the vast pool of aspiring authors seeking a spot in the marketplace as mere sources of income—or, to be even more cynical, ducks in a barrel. In light of the steep costs upper-tier professional services look to extract from authors, combined with the lack of guarantees on any financial returns, and the difficulties of book sales in general, it's no surprise that many authors become financial casualties in the struggle to succeed.

There are far too many horror stories of authors spending tens of thousands of dollars pursuing success, only to fall flat. While some of those stories have their failures rooted in misguided efforts, unreal expectations, and books that lack sufficient quality to stand out in the marketplace, they do allude to an underlying truth. For all the hopes and dreams held by authors—and dangled like so many beckoning apples by marketplace heavyweights—the plain reality is that the book world is a very tough business.

One last issue fledgling authors need to consider is the temptation to engage marketing for a national audience. While any activity in the virtual world effectively plays out to a global audience, this point is more to illustrate the inherent competition of a national marketing campaign. Such efforts come at a high cost to engage a marketing professional and may produce questionable results as you, a fledgling author, fight for attention against authors with known name recognition and perhaps backing by large publishers.

It's important to remember that a national campaign will have a better chance of engaging and succeeding with promotional targets once an author has developed local marketing success. Local support takes effort to build, but it provides an author with the crucial element of *momentum* that can then propel a national marketing push. While there's a definite draw to use the "go big or go home" mentality, and engage a national effort right out of the publication gate, keep in mind that the promotional targets of such an effort will be choosing between known authors versus unknown authors. In such a climate, and given that most promotional entities look to *join* rather than *build* market momentum, unknown authors have little chance of gaining the national attention they desire.

Now that we've looked at some of the harshness of the marketing world, let's put aside the potential negativity and get back to being positive. Marketing is a challenge. In comparison to marketing, publication is easy. Publication has the benefit of providing a concrete sense of accomplishment in the form of a published book. Marketing, on the other hand, is always an open question, and it's this inherent uncertainty that makes marketing both the most difficult and most rewarding aspect of a book's life.

Marketing fundamentals, part one: author branding and author platform

Too MANY AUTHORS OVERLOOK AN essential concept of the publishing world, and that is to think of their books as a business. In the business world, economic entities divide their public awareness into two categories: their *brand* and their *product*.

How does this translate in the publishing world? As the author of one or more books or short stories, you're a *brand,* the common element from which your written titles—your *products*—originate. Think of it in the same way as a car company, with the company being the brand and the individual car models it sells as the products.

It may seem a semantic runaround, but this is the lingo of marketing. Authors who don't understand it, or fail to gain awareness, risk losing the full advantage of opportunities. Everything accomplished during an author's publication career needs to be viewed from the perspective of brand and product so that the proper promotional statements are used in the proper settings. How promotional statements are worded decide whether they apply to author brand or author product.

These ideas tie into the concept of the *author platform.* This too can sound like semantic mumbo-jumbo to authors who don't fully understand how marketing works. The author platform is a concise statement or statements that provide an author with a distinct identity, usually encapsulated in a platform tag line. Your tag line relates to another marketing term, the *elevator pitch,* that is, how you would describe yourself or your book to an industry professional during a thirty second elevator ride.

I will use my own literary credentials to make examples. In summary, I have published three books: *Remnant, Oddities & Entities,* and *Prism.* The books have unanimously positive reviews and have been recognized with numerous national book awards. My publications span numerous genres.

How does this translate into marketing terms?

My platform statement:

> *"Roland Allnach, multi-award winning author of the strange and surreal."*

This one short sentence conveys credibility in the *multi-award winning* clause and implies that I've published genre material outside mainstream fiction with the clause *strange and surreal.*

This sums up my brand.

When talking about my books—my products—the statements are more specific:

> "*Roland Allnach, author of the science fiction anthology, Remnant, recipient of four national book awards.*

> "*Roland Allnach, author of the supernatural and horror anthology, Oddities & Entities, recipient of seven national book awards.*"

> "*Roland Allnach, author of his third award-winning anthology, Prism, an exploration of diverse genres and literary forms.*"

Notice that each short statement not only touts my awards but also mentions a specific book and a few words to identify its content for readers. With *Prism*, the additional notation that it's my third book is to help build my credibility as a more established author.

For many authors these statements will take time to assemble. They also require regular updates as the author's publication credits evolve. Even authors at the top of the market modify their branding statement to revolve around their most recent publication. Authors need to remember that they are individuals among a vast number of fellow authors in the publication world. Effective branding, product, and platform statements are fundamental tools in an author's marketing toolkit.

While these statements may seem boisterous in comparison to the sterile humility authors are compelled to employ in every other phase of their publication efforts, the reality is that society gets bombarded with these statements day in and day out. Only the top A-list people in any field have the implicit name recognition to transcend the necessity of these statements. For the rest of the world these statements are standard practice.

As an experiment, watch any news channel and listen when guests are introduced. There will always be a name followed by a very quick description. This description is often taken as a way to lend context to the guest's background and relevance to the segment, but it is in fact a branding statement. Would a viewer be more inclined to listen to statements on foreign policy from a guest who was introduced as a former member of the State Department or from a guest who was introduced as a head chef? It's not to diminish the chef, but the background of "chef" doesn't hold relevance to a discussion on foreign policy.

Likewise, an author needs an effective branding statement during marketing activities so that readers understand the author's position in the market. When I do any market activities, my marketing copy includes my branding statement, "Roland Allnach, multi-award-winning author of the strange and surreal." Whenever I discuss my books, I mention their genre and the fact they've won numerous awards.

One of the obstacles authors encounter in crafting their brand, platform, and marketing statements is the misconception of "bragging." As I said above, and as authors learn with any experience inside the publication process, when submitting material to short story markets, editors, publishers, or agents, the professional expectation is that all correspondence—such as cover or query letters—is written only with relevant, objective statements. In this phase of an author's activities, none of the recipients want to hear claims of how exciting, thrilling, or compelling past or present works may be for readers. Awards are objective, as is a noteworthy sales statement.

On the other hand once the author bridges from publication to promotion, the narrative of marketing material is much different. Awards are objective but need to be touted, as well as sales, but now the author has full right to tout favorable reviews, rave quotes from readers, and can include those subjective descriptive statements that would be completely out of place both contextually and professionally on the business side of submissions.

Remember that an author is the best and often sole champion for a book's success. It's not easy to acquire a comfort level for marketing and promotional talk that strikes the right mark between bland and bragging. The difficulty of that balance is why the publishing world has marketing firms and experts. Nevertheless, authors still need to understand that the proper use of branding statements, platform identity, and product statements play a significant role in the long-term process of building recognition.

Marketing fundamentals, part two: media marketing material

Once a book is published, an author will need to look into preparing three vital pieces of marketing material. These consist of the *book fact sheet*, the *book excerpt*, and the *press kit*. These will be used by the author during promotional efforts and may even be requested by various marketing outlets prior to a marketing effort. Among these three tools is an item often overlooked for its very simplicity: the bookmark, perhaps the most basic advertisement tool available to an author. Last but not least, with everything else in place, it's a good idea to consider a book trailer video.

Book Fact Sheet

This is a one-sided page to represent your book. It will include a brief synopsis, a list of relevant awards, perhaps a few review quotes, technical book information, such as page count, print format, ISBN, publication date and publisher name, and if space allows, a brief author bio. An image of the book cover should also be included. It's a lot of information to fit on a page. Edit carefully to include the essentials without crowding the page.

Book Excerpt

The excerpt is just that: typically, the first twenty or so pages of content. The book excerpt should in some way capture the essence of the book without divulging its most intimate secrets. Often this will indeed consist of the opening pages where the narrative is geared to those who by default are unfamiliar with the rest of the book. However, this isn't an ironclad rule. In some cases excerpts can supersede the need to make contextual sense by instead conveying a section of particular descriptive or narrative impact. If such a section is used for an excerpt, the author should look to the content of the excerpt for its ability to stand on its own. An excerpt so far removed from the ability to explain itself will do little to represent a book, no matter the impact of its descriptive or narrative elements.

Even greater care needs to be exercised when producing a book excerpt for an anthology. Depending on the number of pieces within the anthology, the author needs to consider whether to utilize short sections of each story or use longer sections of fewer stories that depict the overall theme. Either practice will by necessity shorten the individual excerpts, so the author will have to be more attentive to the same considerations for a longer excerpt one would use from a book.

Press Kit

This is a multi-page document. The first page is a cover sheet resembling the book fact sheet, winnowed to an even tighter format to allow a listing of the press package contents. After the cover page, include tear sheets of favorable book reviews, any notable press releases announcing awards, book launches, or anything touting the book. The press kit does not include a book excerpt.

❋

Of these three pieces, the book fact sheet will find the most use. Include a fact sheet when sending queries for exposure and when sending out copies for review, particularly to bloggers. It's the one piece of paper that can be used to give a snapshot of a book.

While fact sheets, excerpts, and press packages provide a rather formal way to present a book, perhaps the most common and accessible way to present a book is through the use of bookmarks. The humble bookmark can be viewed as an author's business card. There's ample advice for authors to have business cards as well, but there's a difference. Business cards are a convenient exchange of information for professional interactions, whereas bookmarks are a functional exchange of information between authors and readers. Bookmarks, after all, have a readily identifiable use in the minds of readers.

Bookmarks

When designing a bookmark, one will find about as many pieces of advice as design templates. There are services that will design bookmarks; likewise, authors can save some money by doing the design work on their own. Either way, there are several basic pieces of information a bookmark should include. The front of the bookmark should denote the book title, book cover image, author name, ISBN, notable retail channel(s) and formats—print, Kindle, etc. —a very short synopsis, awards, perhaps a review quote or two, author website, and, if preferred, author email. The back of the bookmark can be used to support past publications; as space provides, and include cover images, synopses, reviews, and awards.

It's not difficult to design a bookmark using online printing services. Websites such as Printrunner.com utilize flexible templates or a completely open format, providing authors with simple click, cut, and paste functions. There are also choices for bookmark size, gloss or matte finish, and cardstock weight. In the same manner, there are even more options for business card designs, including the aforementioned Printrunner. com and the well-known Vistaprint.com. Cost will vary, depending on whether or not cards have print on both sides; in either case, bulk ordering of bookmarks or business cards, typically done in lots of one hundred or more, will keep the cost at several cents per individual item.

Book trailer videos

While the above-mentioned marketing materials can be had for little or no cost, book trailer videos are a different matter. Depending on how fancy a production, the cost of a video can be minor or substantial. With that in mind, at the same time it's important not to underestimate the impact of an effective video.

Perhaps the best way to conceptualize a trailer video is to think of how movie trailers are put together. In many ways they seek to accomplish the same goal of enticing an audience with a relatively short capture of viewers' attention. A good foundation for a book trailer concept is to build on the book's tag line and summation, content that was already created for the back cover. Such wording has the same intention of grabbing reader attention with a handful of words, so it can translate well—if not directly—into a video outline.

When it comes to producing a video, all options will be separated by cost. At the lowest end of the cost spectrum are do-it-yourself options such as available at the site Animoto.com. This service allows you to use templates for building a presentation from standard photo (.jpg) images and allows for creation of text cells between the images. You can preview, edit, add music, and then upload to Youtube for sharing and reference in marketing efforts. For more professional sound tracks, investigate licensed musical scores from an expansive source site such as Mediamusicnow.co.uk. After a small fee—around $25—you can obtain licensed permission to a soundtrack.

Moving up the cost scale will involve hiring a person or service to produce the video for you. Videographers come in different stripes, so it's best to do your research and ensure the candidate not only has some experience with book trailers, but that prior videos are acceptable to your tastes and marketing goals. How much a produced video will cost depends on the depth of the production. Voice-overs can add to the cost, as well as possible live action appearances and more complicated video effects. In essence, the more you want, the more you pay.

Videos produced by professionals will obviously have a visual edge over a do-it-yourself video. On the other hand, a do-it-yourself video can be revisited at no cost for additions or updates. At the end of the day, personal economics will most likely be the deciding factor in which route is chosen.

Pundit recommendations: how to keep them in perspective

ONE OF THE MOST CONFOUNDING situations authors face upon their first research into marketing is an overabundance of advice. There are as many opinions as there are authors, and there are as many recipes for successful marketing runs as there are successful marketing runs. There are also many commentators who derive their own promotional efforts by blogging about, and providing, services for marketing efforts. Regardless of any claims that are made, remember that not a single marketing effort comes with a guarantee. On the other hand successful marketing efforts often work by building on some identifiable or discovered facet of the subject book and author.

Blogs, websites, message boards, print magazines, and how-to books are rife with suggestions and standardized approaches for what starting authors should do to open opportunities for success. Unfortunately, almost all these lack one glaring reality check: they often consume more hours than exist in a day. Most often these pundit plans revolve around social media and state daily time minimums an author should invest in various platforms. This can be both daunting and even demoralizing to the starting author, who most likely is in a situation where a job is still being worked to cover living expenses, family time may still be in the picture, and time for writing—no matter how much of a passion—is relegated to a third or lower priority.

As frustrating as this may be, there are still a number of sound advice sources on pragmatic approaches to marketing. Again, they principally involve social media. Why is it that social media seems to lurk at the center of any marketing conversation? The simple answer is that it's *free*. Everyone loves to hear free, and every pundit loves to draw attention with the tired cliché tagline claiming a formula to make a bestseller with zero financial investment. While it's true that such cases happen, they are blown out of proportion compared to the number of authors and books that realize success through hard work and determination.

The publishing industry has a vested interest in this lottery mentality. Pardon the cynicism, but this mentality serves the business interests of several corporate entities in the publishing world—though not necessarily the interest of authors. Publishers enjoy this mentality because it keeps authors submitting books. Agents, as well as editors and marketing professionals, enjoy this mentality for the same reason. Authors may enjoy this mentality for a short time because it seems to keep the door open to quick success.

The truth is there's rarely quick or easy success in the publishing world for the simple reason that the world of books moves slow by nature. Unlike any other creative art form, the world of books has no way to generate immediate interest. Books take time to read, which means readers can only take on so many books at once. By contrast someone can listen to a song or watch a preview for a movie and form an instant opinion far more powerful than even skimming a book can create.

While this may seem a digression, it's an important tangent to keep in mind. It's been said many times previously in this primer, and it needs to be said again: success in the publishing world requires perseverance and patience. Marketing is no different.

In contrast to everything that happens before a book is published, marketing requires experimentation and the willingness to evolve into opportunities that arise. The pre-publication process is ordered in its progression of inspiration, creation, publisher selection, editorial work, and book design. Options exist, but they are kept on a narrow lane in relevance to the book in question. After publication, marketing is an open field. Social media, in particular, offers outlets for every kind of book.

So where does one begin? It is indeed a tough question and again a source of the countless pieces of advice in the publishing world. The best advice, though, is to be practical. Look at what's comfortable for you and what you already possess to promote your writing. If you already have a presence on social media, by all means put it to use. Social media can be a powerful tool, but its sheer number of outlets can dilute an author's time. Time is required to make social media outlets successful. There are quite a few pundits who advise authors to participate in at least four or five social media outlets and devote a minimum of thirty minutes or so a day to each outlet. Combine that with the common advice that an author should write a minimum of several thousand words a day, read the top books within the author's genre, *and* keep tabs on market research, and things escalate into the realm of impossibility.

Yes, it's important to be aware of what books succeed in your genre. It's also important to stay fresh and different rather than emulate a trend. By the time a trend develops in the sales side of the publication world, the agent and publishing side is most likely looking for something else. Yes, it's valuable to do research and be an educated participant in the market.

This does not mean, however, that you need to absorb an encyclopedic knowledge of all things publishing. Yes, it's important to participate in social media, but keep it in practical focus. Choose one or two outlets to start, experiment, and if they seem burdensome or lack comfort, try a different outlet. It may be daunting to look upon all the different outlets available, but turn that around and it becomes an advantage of choice.

At the end of the day, remember the one simple truth of marketing: if you don't promote your book, it will fail. Every book has a built-in sales statistic, and that statistic is zero. Marketing is the only way to change that stark truth. Remember as well that the best joy of an author is to have readers enjoy your book. Without marketing, no one will know your book exists.

Marketing realities of self-, small, and large publishers

IN PART 4, REGARDING NOVELS, there was quite a bit of discussion regarding the contrasting realities between self-, small and large publishers. Some of that discussion tied into marketing because both the perception and the reality for many authors are the decided advantages one can experience when moving up the scale of publishing houses.

For purposes of marketing there's essentially little or no difference between the situation authors face when published by a self- or small publisher. Most small publishers lack the economic resource for publicity efforts and transfer this task to their authors. While these small publishers encourage and often foster promotional groups to aid authors in helping promote each other and the publisher, this can still pose a very uphill battle of recognition for the authors. For marketing to succeed there has to be a ready, willing, and available audience to receive the message. The catch-22 confronted by groups of new or unknown authors is that they promote to build an audience, but until they have an audience, the promotion goes unheard. Outside of pursuing a patient process—perseverance!—there's no open lane of opportunity for authors to pursue.

On the other hand the rise of self-publishers has enabled some companies to offer authors publicity packages in conjunction with publication packages. The various imprints of Author House are probably the most recognizable examples, offering a variety of services from their parent publisher for everything from distribution options all the way to screenplay treatments. Although there's an associated price for each of these services, their availability is at least something to consider, and their openness to books and authors outside the imprints makes them options to consider for those willing to invest.

Moving up the scale of publishers, things change among the larger publishers. While they, as well, have dialed back their marketing efforts and offloaded much of the responsibility onto their authors, large publishers still hold the keys to opportunities smaller publishers and self-publishers simply don't possess. Furthermore, when a large publisher decides to put its muscle behind a particular book and anoint it as a potential winner in the marketplace, many doors can open for premium exposure.

This may seem an unfair advantage for those fortunate enough to land with a large publisher. In a way it is, but that's the reality of the marketplace. In another way it's not, because an author who starts with a large publisher might fail to appreciate these opportunities, as opposed to an author who has worked in the marketing trenches.

Regardless of where a book's publisher sits on the size scale, there's a definite lean in marketing options and audience interest toward recent publications. In this sense time is an inescapable equalizer. Indeed, many market analysts quote six months as the premium sales opportunity for a newly published book. Some extend that window out to a year, but few will consider the average book a worthwhile marketing premium outside that time frame. Opportunities still exist, and the author should never relent, but the book will no longer be a "fresh item."

Make the most of what's free

Although marketing can constitute a major expense in the post-publication arc of a book's life, the good news is that there are some valuable promotional tools that are in fact free.

In the modern publishing world it's hard to find a book that isn't listed with Amazon. One of the conveniences of Amazon is that it allows authors to set up a free author page as part of Amazon's Author Central program. After a simple, straightforward initial set up—it can be done with a pre-existing Amazon shopping account—authors will have access to the coveted synopsis and description areas of their books' product pages. In this area authors can use Author Central to custom craft the book summary, cite awards, quote reviews, and include an author bio. Author Central also provides authors with a dedicated author page where readers can see all the author's published material, in all formats, in one place.

Author Central has tools to track sales. While this sounds enticing, it has limitations. Kindle sales, particularly if your book is done through Amazon's Kindle Direct, will be tracked in an accurate and timely manner. For all other sales, particularly print sales, sales statistics can experience lengthy delays before posting. In short don't be dismayed if sales of which you are personally aware take weeks or months to appear. The reasons for this are part of the complicated interaction between book wholesalers, Amazon's own inventory and fulfillment service, and the tracking systems used between these entities.

Other free sources with good market presence can be utilized through the community book services of Goodreads, LibraryThing, and AuthorsDen. While AuthorsDen starts as a free service, however, its more robust features are only available with paid membership. There are many other sites in addition, but these three are perhaps the most recognizable. Functions are simple and similar across services, requiring authors to create an account, import published titles, and create an author bio. There are some specific differences between services, but in general they allow authors to post reviews for books they've read, which can allow readers to see what an individual author reads and how the author views other titles in the marketplace. A large factor of the services is the ability—and perhaps the necessity—of authors to build an online personality through posts of reviews, integrated blog posts, reader forums, author-sponsored forums, and reader groups.

Services such as Goodreads, LibraryThing, and AuthorsDen also offer more conventional marketing services. These will most likely entail direct costs—ad placement—as well as indirect costs—time and giveaway copies. Such endeavors can have their rewards however. LibraryThing in particular heavily promotes its author giveaway service within its reader community.

The eight hundred pound gorilla of free marketing is, of course, social media. I only return to this topic for the use of social media in conjunction with efforts made on other free services. The biggest challenge as a newly published author or a fledgling author is simply to get noticed. By utilizing some of the free services in tandem with social media, even a new author has the potential to reach an audience. There's no guarantee the audience will respond; however, the important factor is to get in front of the audience. It may take multiple efforts to gain any notice, so once again perseverance comes into play.

How does one put it together? Consider this example in which an author who has accounts at both Goodreads and Facebook launches a virtual book tour for a new title. All the services discussed in this section allow authors to post events and news. The author can benefit from the included advertisement of the virtual book tour coordinator, free exposure by utilizing the targeted reading communities of Goodreads, and broadcast yet another message on Facebook. Each review garnered from the book tour can be quoted in new postings to keep the thread alive, with the quotations and hyperlinks to the reviews included. In addition glowing review quotes can be added to the book's product page on Amazon via Author Central.

Free marketing can be both labor and time intensive, but an author would be remiss to neglect its opportunities.

Virtual book tours and blog promotions

THE INTERNET IS POPULATED WITH a diverse, vibrant community of bloggers willing to review and advertise books. This mutually beneficial relationship provides bloggers with material to satisfy the consistent demand for fresh postings and authors with channeled audiences ready for book exposure.

As with so many other options when utilizing the Internet for marketing, there's a free way to approach bloggers for reviews, guest posts, or interviews. Most blogs that consider books and authors have a page for submission instructions, along with a somewhat disheartening statement that there's no guarantee if or when a book will be featured. With this in mind it's no secret that coordinating exposure on several blogs is next to impossible. That's where the virtual book tour steps into the picture.

Virtual book tours are a paid service for authors to shop their books to readers. A virtual book tour, or VBT, is arranged by a coordinating service. The author pays the service in exchange for the service coordinating with bloggers to host virtual book tour "stops." These stops can include a book *reveal*, consisting of a cover image, excerpt, and author bio, a text interview, an author guest post, or a book review. The cost of a VBT will vary depending on the number of tour stops, the popularity of individual blogs on the tour, and whether or not the stops will be centered on reviews. Tours that center around reviews may incur extra expense due to the time commitment of the blogger; conversely, tour stops that consist of text interviews, reveals, or author guest posts only require the labor of the blogger to post information supplied by the author or VBT service.

Tour coordinators offer different levels of service. Some coordinators, such as TLC Book Tours, only offer tours with reviews and, thereby, call for a higher expense. Other coordinators, such as Pump Up Your Book, offer a suite of services that include not only tours of varying lengths, but associated promotional services such as book announcements or cover reveals. With careful planning an author can utilize these pre-publication promotional services to build "buzz" on blogs before the actual book tour begins. This can be of particular importance for successive titles in a series of books so that readers are made aware of a new installment. Even for a single book in the post-publication phase, this is a strategy authors may want to consider.

As with anything else related to marketing and publishing, authors bear the responsibility of research. There are tour coordinators who specialize in different genres and thereby cater to blogs who expose a book to an audience of similar interest. There are also coordinators who utilize blogs with large numbers of followers who are not book-centric; these blogs are often generalized review sites that feature a range of consumer products in addition to books. The audience may not be specific to books, yet the audience may be much larger.

The most important part of a blog tour is for the author to participate. One of the fundamentals of marketing is that if an author doesn't show interest in a book, then readers won't be inclined to show interest in a book. In addition to a polite response thanking a blogger for a post, the author should take care to follow all the blog posts of a tour to respond to reader interest. Author accessibility has been shown over and over as a potentially important factor in the purchase decision of readers.

Claim your own corner of cyberspace: build a website and/or blog

Social media and social services can be valuable assets for an author's footprint in the virtual world, but they have one thing in common: as an author, you're only one part of something you can't control. For a truly individualized presence in the virtual world, an author has to consider a website and/or a blog.

Before jumping into this discussion, it's important to point out that no matter what type of Internet presence is chosen—whether it be through social media, blogs, a website, or a combination of the three—every author should have a public email address that can be disclosed for promotional materials. If security is a concern, professional or private interactions can be handled with a separate email account. Nevertheless, between an author's Internet provider and outside services such as Google, Yahoo, and countless others, establishing a public email account is a simple task to complete. Once the account is established it should be referenced in all promotional information, including a blog or website.

Authors courting small publishers will often find that authors are expected—if not required—to already have either a blog or website to use as a foundation for the inevitable marketing responsibilities the author will face. Remember that with small publishers, as opposed to most self-publishers, the publisher has the discretion whether or not to accept the author's book for publication. Publishers may think twice about an author who has no marketing plan or market presence on which to build.

Let's take a look at websites and blogs on their own merits.

Blogs

As opposed to websites, creating a blog is a painless process. There are numerous free blog hosts to use, with Google's Blogger perhaps the most prominent. To make matters of greater ease, there's also a wide selection of reference and help material both in print and online geared toward blogging in general and the mechanics specific to respective hosts. Technicalities aside, the typical blog hosting service will offer templates that quickly allow an author to build a blog site, along with a straightforward control panel to update the blog. Hosts such as Google also offer a variety of ways to monitor the blog's statistics and even monetize the blog through ad posting. In general though, author sites are not the best place for ad banners. You don't want a visitor coming to your blog, seeing an attractive ad, and then immediately leaving to another site.

Arguably, the greatest strength of a blog is its interactive nature. Without getting lost in a lengthy technical discussion on how to manage a blog, suffice it to say there are numerous tools available to make the most of building a blog's presence. Blogs can be linked to each other, posts can be shared, and reader comments can all help to raise the blog's prominence in search engines. Proper and efficient use of highly searched terms in the first two or three lines of a blog post can help increase visibility on search engines.

Blogs allow for a natural, personal way for people to interact on the Internet. If you're unfamiliar with blogging, think of your blog posts as private social media threads on your own slice of the Internet. You can establish both the intent of your blog and, more importantly, your own fair usage rules, that is, what kinds of comments you'll accept. Comments are managed behind the scenes by the use of mediation settings in the blog's control panel. On the public side, acceptable comment rules are set forth by adding a Policy page to the blog to serve as your rulebook.

So how should an author structure a blog? Opinions vary on this issue. Some authors will maintain a blog specific to a single book while others will maintain a single blog with separate pages on the blog for each book title. The main page of the blog is then a general posting area.

This is a simpler set-up, as it only requires the maintenance of one blog with centralized information. On this format, at minimum the blog will consist of its main page, one page for each published book, a policy page, and an author bio page with additional links—website, social media, etc.

There are numerous pieces of advice from pundits on how expansive an author's blogging presence should be, but it's important to keep things in perspective. In the same way social media can be overwhelming, likewise remember that as a new or fledgling author, you want a blog that will work comfortably for you and serve your burgeoning needs. It's better to go a little simpler to start, so that you can keep up with the demands of a blog, rather than to create a wide platform and fall behind. Keep in mind that as your audience grows, so too your blogging efforts can grow.

As posts are created remember to use the host service's control panel to place tags on the posts, and then add a tag directory to the main page of the blog. Don't worry; this is far easier to do than it might sound. This allows visitors to easily search posts based on an area of interest. If a visitor wants to read reviews of your books, and you've tagged every post regarding reviews with a review tag, the visitor can simply click the review tag from the home page directory and the blog will sort and display all the relevant posts.

To be successful with a blog, it must be updated on a regular basis. Time commitment will be the single biggest challenge of running an author blog. Maintaining an active blog requires not only posting about your books and writing but also things outside of your publishing pursuits or perhaps related to publication in general. Consider the 80-20 rule: 80% of an author's social posts should be general interest, while the remaining 20% of posts can be used for author promotion. Part of a blog's atmosphere is to build an online personality through various posts. For visitors to follow a particular blog, they'll want to see something more than an endless stream of thinly veiled book advertisements. A good way to add diversity to a blog is to become a blog tour host, if time provides. All VBT coordinators have applications on their websites for those interested in hosting blog tour stops.

For all a blog's strengths, however, it's important for those who utilize blogs to understand that they don't own the name of their blog, its web address, or its graphical appearance. The only thing the blogger "owns" on a blog is the text content itself. I've seen a few horror stories of bloggers who either lost their provider or had their blog pulled by a hosting service. In the blink of an eye, the bloggers are at a complete loss to rebuild the search rankings and subscriber base that took so long to build. While it's unusual for a hosting service to shut down a blog, it's less unusual for a hosting service to go out of business or be bought by another company. The decision of a hosting service to pull a blog can be quite subjective and almost impossible to argue. Although it's a somewhat remote possibility for an author blog, it's something authors should remember.

As the saying goes, don't put all your eggs in one basket.

Websites

The world of website building can be quite different from that of blogging. While there's a wide choice of sites to help build and host a blog for free, website construction can incur minor to significant expense.

Setting up a website involves three basic steps: selecting a hosting service, selecting a web authoring application, and creating content.

As with blog hosts, there are numerous sites that offer web hosting. Most work on a model wherein they offer monthly or yearly hosting charges. The fee can vary based on the amount of help the hosting service offers in the actual creation of the site, but we'll get into that in a little bit. In many ways there's little difference in the hosting service of these sites; they will assist you in registering your domain—your website name, such as www.rolandallnach.com—and assign an IP address so that your site is visible to the rest of the Internet.

At this stage of web construction, it's important to read the fine print on the hosting agreement, namely, to be certain that you retain ownership of the website's domain name. Every hosting service will register your domain name; this is essential to having your site be part of the Internet. However, registering your domain name does *not* mean you own the domain name. This will be specifically defined in the hosting agreement. If there's no clause defining the domain ownership, contact the hosting service's support system to clarify this issue.

Why is domain ownership important? Once you own the domain, no one else can use it unless you specifically sell it. If another party owns the domain name, it's tied into their business interest, not yours, and they have the discretion whether or not to sell your domain name if an outside party makes a purchase offer. Once your domain name is sold, your website effectively ceases to exist until you register a new domain name, at which point you can upload the old site to the new domain. Unfortunately, at that point all your search optimization will be lost. In most cases this is an improbable occurrence, but the only safeguard is to be sure of domain ownership.

Once a hosting service is selected, the next step will be to build a site. This can be done through several means. The simplest and least expensive way is to use a hosting service that offers site templates upon which you insert your content. The compromise for simplicity is the risk of having an aesthetically generic site. The middle option in cost, but perhaps highest in labor, is to purchase a web-authoring application and create the site on your own. This will provide the ultimate in customization at the compromise of time and a learning curve to use the application. Fortunately, most authoring applications these days don't require any knowledge of HTML coding—the computer language of the Internet—and use simplified copy and paste, what-you-see-is-what-you-get—WYSIWYG—functionality.

The most expensive option for site design is to hire a web designer. While this may provide the most professional website in terms of look and functionality, the cost can be steep, ranging from several hundred to several thousand dollars. In addition there may be ongoing expense involved whenever the website needs to be updated.

So how often should a website get updated? At least monthly, which is why some web design services have monthly fees. On the ease-of-use side, some web design services also provide hosting so that they become one-stop solutions.

There are several basic ingredients to an author website. As with blogs there will be a home page, a page for each published book or book series, including purchase links, an author bio page, and something often overlooked, a media page. The media page is a website's central store of promotional material for the author and his or her published books; in short, think of a media page as a central locale for author platform, brand, and product. It should include downloadable press packages, fact sheets, and excerpts in a convenient file format, such as Adobe Acrobat pdf.

As a side note, don't be dismayed by the prospect of working with different file formats for your media documents. While word processor files are the standard when working behind the scenes on publication efforts, they are rarely used for documents offered as website downloads. For this usage, Adobe Acrobat pdf files are the standard. Aside from their widespread accessibility via the free Acrobat Reader, pdf files are also more secure than generic word processor files. Fortunately, modern word processors such as Microsoft Word can save files to pdf format. In addition, there are inexpensive online conversion utilities to convert Word files to pdf and vice versa. The most notable of these—surprise—is available from Adobe itself.

The general style aesthetic with websites is to have a favorable blend of blank space and text. It can be a tough balance to achieve for an author website, where everything is supposed to focus on the written word. Some common sense can be a useful guide for this delicate design process, in that the same general rules for good narrative form can be applied to good web form. Text should flow, sections of text should be relevant without word bloat, and the quality of the text should not be overlooked. Remember, the idea of an author's website is to promote that author's *writing.*

The tone of the text itself can vary. Some authors prefer a more sterile third person style while others prefer a more personable, casual first person style. On my site I vary between the two, using a third person professional tone for marketing, while moving to first person when relating direct experience, personal opinion, or creative background on my fiction.

Due to limitless design options, a website can reflect an author's personality or literary tastes even more so than a blog. If you have both a website and a blog, don't forget to cross-reference their pages with hyperlinks. While a website lacks the instant feedback exchange of a blog, a website can be set up with regular news posts. In this regard a website is no different than a blog; either can provide a negative impression without signs of recent activity. However, the periodicity of updates for a website can be much less than a blog. To foster a blog, it needs to be updated at least weekly, and some advise to post on a daily basis. On a website a monthly news update will suffice.

Meet your audience: book signings and interviews

MANY PEOPLE WHO DECIDE TO pursue publication share a dream of sitting on the author's side of a book signing or interview. Recognition as an author isn't about vanity; it's an acknowledgment of the time, sacrifice, and accomplishment that goes with writing and publishing a book. However, recognition can't happen in a vacuum. Public events are fantastic ways to get out of that vacuum, gain exposure, and contact potential readers.

Although both signings and interviews are perhaps the most public aspects of an author's publishing life, they are somewhat different. Let's take a look at each.

Book signings

Book signings provide authors direct interaction with people and the opportunity for direct sales. There's no denying the impact a favorable interaction with a potential reader can have on the sale of a book. Even so, signings are not entirely about sales. Rather, they allow authors to humanize themselves to readers. Instead of existing as a name on a book cover, the author has the opportunity to manifest as a flesh-and-blood person. Likewise it allows authors the almost priceless opportunity to listen to the interests of readers and gauge reader response to subject matter contained in the author's book or books. This can be valuable reference material for the author to discern how well his or her titles are meshing with market interest or perhaps indicate to the author what might be the next popular topic to pursue for a writing project.

Demeanor is crucial at the author table. As an author you'll meet a wondrous array of people, some who are receptive, some who are not. Signings are a benefit of publication, so be upbeat and open to discussion.

Keep in mind that the point of publication was to present your creative work to readers. No matter the case, remember to be polite, gracious, and don't take any comments as personal affronts. While some visitors may test your patience, don't lose patience on any count. A visitor's negative experience at a table can blow up to something much larger, thanks to the very same social media channels an author employs to build good favor. Perhaps the only comment an author can make is to ask someone lingering at the table to make room for other visitors, and this should be done with the utmost tact.

When attending a signing event, remember to present yourself well. If possible stand rather than sit, as sitting can be viewed as non-receptive. Also it's easier to be seen when standing. Keep your table organized at events that require you to process your own sales transactions. A cash box is an inexpensive and easy way to secure loose bills, receipts, and small items, whereas electronic transactions can be handled via plug-in smart phone credit card readers available through services such as Paypal, Square, and Amazon.

A sample copy of each book should be available for visitors to peruse and an email sign-up sheet should be available to collect these potentially valuable sales contacts. Bookmarks should also be available; invite visitors to take bookmarks whether or not they show interest. A bookmark has the potential of turning into a sale after the event. If a visitor isn't sold on a print copy, gently remind them if the book is available in digital or audio format.

Opinions vary among authors and pundits regarding the best way to attract attention for an author's table. At the least there should be some type of stand-up display similar to a book fact sheet. This feature should display the book cover, a very brief synopsis, a few review quotes, any award citations, and different media options such as print, Kindle, Audible, etc. While such displays work well once someone is at the table, they won't be able to engage people from a distance. The best way to bridge the proximity gap is with a banner.

Banners are available in three principal forms: stand-up, pull-up, and table. Stand-up banners are placard-sized displays supported by a stand.

Inexpensive, lightweight, and easy to carry, they offer indoor ease at the sacrifice of outdoor inconvenience. The slightest breeze can send them flying and, even when secured, they can be damaged by a light wind. Stand-up banners also consume table space, which may be limited.

In comparison to stand-up banners, pull-up banners offer more display space, free up table clutter, and offer superior visibility. On the downside they have the highest purchase price and increased susceptibility to wind. Except for a very calm day, pull-up banners are limited to indoor use.

Table banners, on the other hand, offer perhaps the best practicality. They provide more space than a stand-up display, price much lower than a pull-up display, and remain secure while hanging from the front of a signing table. A pair of inexpensive work clamps from a hardware store can anchor the banner to your table. As with stand-up banners, table banners are lightweight and can be rolled up for storage in a mailing tube. Visibility, though, is somewhat less than the higher stance of stand-up and pull-up banners. Nevertheless, they are the best overall choice for both indoor and outdoor events.

Costs can vary depending on the materials used for banners and their respective sizes. For general reference, a typical 2 by 3 foot stand-up display will cost $20 to $30, a similarly sized table banner will cost in the neighborhood of $40, and a pull-up display can easily cost $100 or more. In addition to the initial cost, keep in mind that as your publishing efforts expand, you might have to replace a banner with an updated version. At that point a pricey expenditure can end up as a lost expenditure.

Regardless of shape or style, a banner should include your platform statement and/or a catchy tagline identifying the genre of your writing. Be sure the banner print is large enough to be read from six to ten feet away. People will consider this a safe "hovering" distance as they make their decision whether or not to approach your table. Banners can be easily designed and purchased from services such as Vistaprint and Printrunner.

There are some who recommend offering a candy bowl to entice visitors; others recommend advertising a discount for autographed copies sold at the signing. A sample copy mired by sticky fingers can be a turn-off to subsequent visitors; likewise, a deep discount smacks of desperation. At the most a book discount should eliminate the distributor cost, allowing a roughly 25% discount—and don't forget to remind visitors that you'll be glad to sign the book. After all, it is a book *signing*. In the end what an author is allowed to do will certainly depend on a venue's rules, so take care to check before setting up.

How do you ensure a good turnout for a book signing? Once again the golden answer is promotion. The exact process will depend on the type of signing event. For a single author signing at a venue such as a bookstore, the venue, hopefully, will provide direct advertisement for the signing. For tag-along events, such as a signing table at a craft fair, the venue's advertisement will promote the event but not necessarily an author signing. In either case the burden once again falls on the author to employ standard marketing means to promote turnout. Use of social media, book community sites—Goodreads, AuthorsDen, LibraryThing, etc.—and press releases are all options.

A book signing is no different than any other promotional or marketing effort in that there are no guarantees. Some signings will go well; others will consist of several hours sitting mostly alone at your table. The difference between these outcomes varies on a number of factors, most often the event turnout based on the event's promotion.

Either way—successful or not—consider this basic truth: while an event might not have the desired results, staying at home guarantees zero results. You became an author to share your stories. Any opportunity to connect with readers is a gift.

Interviews

Another wonderful way to humanize your presence to the public at large is through an interview. Interviews can be done in written form, podcast, Internet or terrestrial radio, and through television. Aside from the written format, interviews are either performed with scripted questions or improvised as part of a dynamic conversation between author and interviewer.

No matter the format, remember that an interview is a marketing tool and therefore a way to present your marketing points. While scripted interviews provide control over the questions, and therefore the content of your replies, even in improvised interviews be sure to work your talking points into your answers. These should include your platform statement and any product points for your book or books.

The reality of most interviews is that the interviewer may not have read your book. In these cases the interviewer will rely on supporting marketing material, such as a press kit, provided prior to the interview. The interview will most likely follow scripted questions provided by the author, with the interviewer able to exercise an option of additional questions, depending on the flow of the interview. For improvised interviews the interviewer will most likely read the book and then work from a combination of interviewer questions and generalized questions that touch upon the marketing aspects of the book.

It's important to be relaxed during an interview. Even in a written interview, it's rather easy to discern someone comfortable with discussion from someone who's guarded. As daunting as an interview may be, remember one crucial factor: you are the author, and no one can possibly know your material better than you. A second crucial point is to be honest. This doesn't mean to divulge your most intimate secrets but more so to be true to your material and yourself. Not only will these perspectives allow you to maintain consistency with your answers, but they will assuage some of the anxiety that can come with an interview.

When doing an interview, keep your demeanor in mind. Be personal, connect with the interviewer, and convey enthusiasm for your material. No one wants to listen or watch someone who displays little emotional range or who speaks in a monotone. As with anything else, if you as the author don't express interest in your material, you can't expect anyone else to be interested.

The most notable *faux pas* of an interview is the dreaded trinity of "um," "uh," and lingering silence. If you don't have an instant answer to a question, reiterate what was asked and start answering as best as possible. An answer that strays from the actual question isn't a problem so long as it offers content of interest. This is particularly true with improvised interviews where there is no fixed script.

Last but not least don't forget proper etiquette. Authors should thank their interviewers at the start and close of an interview. At the end of the interview, be ready to talk about future writing plans or events—"plugs"—if the interviewer offers this opportunity. It may seem to go without saying, but other than a glaring factual error, do not contest the interviewer, just the same as you should not contest a reviewer.

As with any other marketing endeavor, remember your promotional exercises before the interview. In the same way a venue has a vested interest in promoting a book signing, so too an interviewer has a vested interest in promoting an interview. This may entail generalized promotion for the interview host, such as a "tune in tomorrow" type of statement, or a more pointed promotion such as, "tune in next week when I'll be speaking with author Jane Smith." Aside from these intrinsic promotional efforts, the burden will be on the author to get the word out. Once again start with the basics—social media, community book-reading sites, and consider a press release.

Press release, you ask? Drum roll ... it's segue time!

The fine print on press releases

As TIME-HONORED STANDBYS OF THE media world, press releases are used to disseminate timely information to garner interest for a particular topic. From the publishing perspective such information might include an award announcement, pre-publication buzz, speaking event, etc.

A press release is only as good as its distribution. To understand how to compare values with press releases, one needs to understand how the distribution model works. Press releases can be distributed across a home site, distributed to partner sites, or distributed across national news wires. The relative cost of a press release is related to these distribution systems, with home sites being of little or no cost, partner sites consisting of mid-range cost for distribution—$100-$300—and national news wire access being the most expensive, typically starting at $600 and going up from there.

Free press releases are limited to the origin home site and rely on visitors to the home site to view the press release. If visitors find it of interest, they can then reference the release to help distribute the news. While this may be a free service model, its limited distribution handicaps the very point of the release, which is to disseminate timely information. This is similar to the social networking model of publicity where one relies on the burgeoning interest of various parties to raise awareness. Remember, however, that the idea of a release is to get out a timely announcement to generate interest. In the world of press releases, time is everything. A press release that's a few days old is already ancient news.

Mid-range cost press releases are often posted to a variety of press release origin sites, as well as the host site and its affiliates. While this is a much more thorough distribution out of the box, it's limited to the audience already in place at the host and its affiliate sites. If you're intended audience is very targeted or narrow in range, and the host site is within that interest range, this is a sweet-spot choice between cost and exposure.

National news wire press releases are the gold standard. These releases are distributed nationally to all major media outlets for their review and possible interest. Typically, when someone at CNN picks up a press release, that person didn't go to a free release website and find the release. The release came across the Associated Press (AP) service direct to CNN's news editors. It's this very scope of reach and access that merits the higher cost of these releases. For the opportunities and exposure they provide, it's certainly an investment to consider if you have something very big to announce.

Regardless of the distribution, understand that there are certain standards in crafting a professional release. A release is really a piece of ad copy, and there's a certain style inherent to ad writing. Services that access national news wires will usually write the release for you; mid-range services will typically write the release if it's in conjunction with some other service; free release services require you to write the release unless you pay a fee to have a writer craft it for you.

If you want to tackle the release on your own, consider these basic standards.

1. Press releases are typically no more than 300-500 words.
2. Try to keep the release limited to one page in length.
3. The release should be written in the present tense. Remember that it's breaking news, and it's ad copy.
4. National news wire services will not accept releases with heavy images or fancy graphics. In fact, no matter the distribution, aside

from a simple letterhead graphic, there shouldn't be any pictures or graphics in the release.

If you're going to invest in a press release, consider hiring someone experienced in ad writing. Just as writing a synopsis or pitch is very different from writing a book, so too ad copy is its own special brand of expression. People go to college to learn this type of writing, so tap that expertise. It may seem excessive, but remember that a press release is also an investment. In the same manner as awards and market reviews, you own the release after its distribution. Releases can serve continued use as part of a book press kit, book pitches, or any other promotional endeavor.

Economic considerations for marketing

THOUGH BY NOW THE FOLLOWING statement might sound like the proverbial broken record, the cold hard truth of the book world is that marketing efforts can be expensive. The irony of the publicity world is that when you most need professional marketing, the cost can be prohibitive, yet once your publishing career is at the point where cost isn't a factor, a publisher may very well cover the expense for you. The publicity industry is built on the notion of contacts, and all the good contacts are of course held at a premium. Furthermore, the art of publicity is something many authors don't understand and aren't prepared to tackle when first published. It's a daunting task requiring patience and persistence to persevere. There go those "p" words again! All of these factors contribute to the existence of publicity professionals.

First, I'd like to return to the realm of "free publicity" through social media. The successes here are often touted, but with a little investigation it's not hard to decipher the apparent ease of social networking success as a lottery mentality. Such success stories are filled with the dreamy portent of great reward with minimal effort, financial and time-wise. Unfortunately, this simply isn't the case.

I should frame everything I'm about to say in the context of my individual situation, which is that I work under a very crowded time schedule. Like most authors, I can't support myself from my writing; rather, I have a job to pay the bills—and support my writing. I also have a family. Add to this some time for sleep—Sleep? What's that?—and there really isn't much time to go around. Being active in social media not only means investing the time to post on respective sites, but also time to follow stories, locate groups that may take interest in your writing, and time spent considering ideas that might draw interest as posts.

My opinion is that social networking has to be taken under advisement. Yes, it can be a very powerful tool to add to your publicity and marketing arsenal. However, I believe it works best when it adds to publicity momentum. In addition keep in mind that many authors will be looking to draw the attention of a potential audience within the same area of interest in which you write. In this perspective the virtual social world is no different than the physical world: when no one knows who you are, they don't know to listen to you; when people do know who you are, they're already listening to you, and you can build on that. How one makes the transition from unknown to known is the result of time and effort spent plugging away with social posts. Networking can also provide great opportunities to link with other people, but once again, they have to be encountered.

So what's the verdict on social networking as a publicity tool? It's a great alternative, but the deferment in financial cost is leveraged against a significant cost in time. Consider it as something to complement traditional publicity efforts, not something to replace those efforts.

With that in mind, sooner or later traditional publicity efforts will have to be engaged. There are numerous publicity firms to choose from, and the prices of services vary widely. In my experience, use an old wisdom as your guide: you get what you pay for. I've seen some ads for publicity services touting prices that are a bare fraction of similar services from other firms. What's the difference?

There are several areas where costs can be cut at great sacrifice to the service you receive. The first way for a firm to trim costs is through press release distribution. Another way to trim costs is through the contact list—does it contain valid publicity leads or just referrals to sites partnered with the publicist? Lastly, consider what you take away from the publicity service; namely, will you keep the media contact list for you to continue to follow? I've seen some firms that retain the list at the conclusion of the service. Reputable services let you keep the media contact list to pursue your follow-ups.

Ah, yes, the follow-up. In most cases the only way to see a contact through to success is through repeated follow-ups. Periodicity of follow-ups is crucial; on one hand, you don't want to nag a contact, while on the other hand, you don't want your query to be forgotten. The proper time balance is open to opinion, but consider a follow-up every two to four weeks as a safe window.

It may seem counter-intuitive to employ the practice of follow-ups after paying for professional marketing services, but it's part of the process. Unless you invest in an expensive—perhaps $3,000 or more—top-tier publicity service, it will be up to you the author to ensure your leads mature. The publicity firm will open the door for you, but you have to invest the time and determination to make something of the contacts you've been given. Once again persistence pays, but remember each lead you see through to maturity is more exposure for your book.

If cost is a primary concern, consider a simple cost/feature calculation by dividing the cost of the publicity service with the number of leads that have matured. With each lead the effective cost per lead decreases. Premium review/promotion packages can run upward of several hundred dollars, so if you invest in a publicity service and see even a few leads through, you'll be in this neighborhood of cost per feature. After that every lead followed to fruition knocks down the amortized cost.

A popular form of publicity involves the aforementioned virtual book tour, or VBT. For blog exposure a VBT can be a great bargain. It's certainly a much better investment than a static ad. Such ads can get quite expensive, regardless of whether it's a print ad or Internet ad such as on Google or Facebook. In either case a reasonable ad budget for a two-line promo that no one might notice could, at the same cost, book a VBT and have your book featured on blogs direct to an audience ready and willing to take an interest in books. A VBT may involve work to prepare interviews and guest blog posts, with the scope of work relative to the scope of the tour. Pick a tour period where you know you'll have time available before and during the tour.

In terms of basic marketing finances, it's best to set aside a few hundred dollars for initial marketing efforts. From this allocation you'll be able to book a preliminary virtual book tour, obtain bookmarks, perhaps purchase some type of promotional banner for book events, and obtain a small stock of author copies for promotional use or direct sales.

To charge or not to charge: gifts and giveaways

AS AN AUTHOR YOU'LL FACE a common situation with your books, particularly so with your first publication. You can't wait to tell everyone that the book is available, especially those who may have supported you emotionally and financially or more. Now comes an interesting question. There are those to whom you may wish to present the book as a gift in appreciation for their support. Where is the line between gifts, charging for copies, and promotional giveaways?

The best advice is to set your borders early. This is the easiest way to avoid awkward and uncomfortable social situations, but it will require commitment. Consider dividing your world into three circles. In the first circle include the people whom you consider the closest in your life. In the second circle include the rest of your private world. The third circle will then consist of the public world at large.

Since my first book I've stuck with my decisions on those borders: I give copies of my books as gifts only to my wife, sons, and parents/ parents-in-law, my first circle. To others in my life, my second circle, I offer the option of a discounted author copy. I also sign the book. To the remaining reading world, the third circle, I use the same price points as I do at author book events.

It can be uncomfortable asking for money. I don't like charging people I know; however, I've found that when I let people know I have copies, they always ask the cost. People who respect the effort to make a book won't haggle. At the same time respect your limits. No one likes a hard sell. A good approach is to let people know copies are available and ask if they're interested in a signed book. Let them look at the book. If they don't ask to buy a copy, thank them for their interest, and let them know they can ask again or buy from traditional channels—Kindle, Nook, print, etc. Again, don't pressure people. Remember as well that in a work environment you don't want to be known as the one running a book business out of the break room.

When it comes to gifting, there's always room for flexibility. If someone extends a particular favor, or extends some extra effort for you, by all means send a gift copy. Remember that people in the publication world love books—that's why most of them are in the publication world. Surprising someone with a signed gift copy can be a gracious and personal sign of appreciation.

Giveaways, on the other hand, are a different matter. Whereas it's up to individual authors to decide where they'll draw the line of gifting among their social circle, book giveaways can be used as a promotional tool. Virtual book tours often use book giveaways to spark interest; likewise, authors can arrange their own giveaways through social media, Goodreads, AuthorsDen, Library Thing, and other services.

Giveaways should entail some type of reciprocation. Blogs often require a visitor to comment on the blog post to be eligible for the giveaway. Giveaways can also be vehicles for recruiting such things as page likes, emails for later promotional purposes, blog follows, and social network follows. In the end, though, a giveaway won't be successful without some promotional commitment. Public response can often mirror an author's effort. Once again, if you as the author do little to talk up a giveaway—in effect, if you show no interest—expect a similar disinterest from the reading world.

Authors can be quite divided on the topic of giveaways. Some feel rather strongly against giveaways on the grounds that it can dissuade actual book sales. After all the work—and potential expense—to see a book through to publication, it can be disheartening to think you now have to hand it over for free.

However, giveaways can involve intangible values beyond a purchase price. A good approach to giveaways is to scale the giveaway to the book's sales, and remember that a giveaway, as with any other promotional effort, doesn't guarantee sales. Remember as well that the giveaway item isn't limited to the book. There are giveaways that offer shopping cards all the way up to Kindle or Nook devices.

If you are yet to prove a sales record, and you're still absorbing the various costs of publication, then you probably shouldn't offer an expensive giveaway. Stick with a copy of your book or a promo bundle of several titles. The value of a giveaway should entice interest, not overshadow the interest value of your book.

A simple, sample marketing plan

After the dust settles from the many considerations of marketing, perhaps the most intimidating step of all is to put together an actual plan. Remember that without some type of marketing effort, a book faces certain oblivion. Any effort, no matter how small, helps a book's chance of success and, thereby, the author's chance of success.

Rudimentary knowledge of the marketing world can allow an unknown, fledgling author to utilize the plan outlined below. It involves some effort, some monetary investment, but it will certainly help spread the word about a book and help expand search links on the Internet. If the response is favorable enough, or if the book finds a core audience, the effort may even realize an appreciable sales return.

So just by assembling and coordinating the basic tools mentioned in the preceding sections, here's a simple, sample marketing plan:

1. *Create pre-buzz on social media.* Utilize your social networking accounts to start spreading word about a book's upcoming publication. Some virtual book tours offer *cover reveal* buzz packages that will tour a book's cover image with a short ad line to help build momentum.

2. *Collect market reviews.* As soon as possible, either through advanced review copies or immediately upon publication, send the book out to at least two or three professional review services. Strongly consider utilizing expedited review packages so that you can have reviews in hand for subsequent marketing steps.

3. *Assemble marketing material.* With a few reviews and perhaps a press release, it's time to put together your basic marketing tools: the book

fact sheet, the book press kit, a book excerpt, bookmarks, and consider a trailer video.

4. *Submit to contests.* If finances allow, consider a few reputable award contests. Remember that contests have rolling publication date requirements, so if you wait too long, the book will no longer be eligible for entry. Also early entry often means discounted costs.

5. *Consider a press release.* A press release of any kind can never hurt. If there's something particularly notable about the book, either from a review, an award, or particular audience interest, sending out a release can further build momentum.

6. *Arrange a virtual book tour (VBT).* With a few reviews and marketing material in hand, consider hiring a VBT service to expose the book to bloggers. This will garner more reviews and help introduce the book to a wider reading world.

7. *Explore book launches and/or book signings.* Tap local libraries and bookstores to see if they are receptive to hosting you and your book for a night with the local community. These events may be more accessible—and more successful—when done in conjunction with a local authors group.

8. *Cross your fingers.* Humor aside, it never hurts to hope. Although luck will always be a welcome companion, opportunities are the result of hard work.

Moving forward: be the proverbial rolling stone

MARKETING PLANS DON'T END WITH one book. It may be a tired analogy, but every marketing effort is indeed another stone in the foundation of your career as an author. Every succeeding publication, and every succeeding marketing effort, will build upon all previous marketing work you've done to establish yourself as an author.

In the past, before the days of the Internet, marketing efforts could disappear from public awareness in the moment of their conclusion. Fortunately, the Internet's endless capacity for storing pages and links allows efforts to live on indefinitely. The proof can be found by a straightforward experiment, and that's to perform a Google search on your name.

Over the course of your marketing and publishing activities, your search hits can expand from a handful to several dozen pages. Every one of those search entries is a possibility for you to be found by a reader.

As such, even if a marketing effort doesn't satisfy its immediate expectations, the links and exposure it creates within the complicated world of search engines and webpage interconnectivity can rapidly expand an author's virtual presence. The deeper the network of one's interconnectivity, the more likely search engines will associate a given author's name or book titles with more generic search terms. This phenomenon is the very basis for businesses that specialize in search engine optimization (SEO).

Nevertheless, every effort you make on behalf of yourself and your book adds not only to your list of credentials but to your experience as an author. Near the beginning of this primer, I posed a simple mental exercise for building confidence. It involved imagining yourself in a room full of people and having someone ask for a show of hands as to who has written a book. Succeeding questions on number of books, awards, and so forth winnows the raised hands.

Now revisit that exercise except for two changes: this time you're sitting in a room of fellow authors, and the people asking the questions on stage are amalgams of readers, interviewers, publishers, and agents. The effect of successive questions can have a more decided effect on your future in the publishing world. Who will these all-important entities choose—the authors who published, then did nothing, or those who stood behind their books, had conviction in their work, belief in their talent, and went out on blog tours, book signings, interviews, and anything else between?

Remember, as an author it took a great deal of emotional and temporal investment to bring a book to life. The only way to justify that effort is to get your book noticed.

In Remembrance of the Typewriter

Wᴴᴇɴ I sᴛᴀʀᴛᴇᴅ ᴡʀɪᴛɪɴɢ, ᴛʜᴇ actual process of assembling words on media was quite different from what it has become today. I handwrote my stories and early books on notepads and then went through the laborious—and now archaic—process of handwritten revisions and edits. Next came an equally laborious and far more tedious exercise of sitting at a typewriter and banging away at the keys. Yes, a mechanical typewriter. No computer, no file to edit on whimsy, no second chance.

In honor of those times, I created the following pieces on my website's For the Writer page, and thought I would reproduce them here as a fitting closure.

✺

Iɴ ᴛʜᴇ ᴏʟᴅ ᴅᴀʏs ᴡᴇ used things called typewriters. Writing was a very tactile process. You had to press a key and wait for the resounding ka-chunk of a lever arm imprinting an engraved character through a moody ink ribbon and onto the page.

Using the *shift* key shifted the drum alignment so that the upper-case character at the top end of the lever struck the ink ribbon rather than the lower-case character. The caps lock just ratcheted the shift key in place.

At the end of a line, you had to grab the return lever and give it a good cross to bring the carriage back to the left margin—origin of the *return* key, before it lost relevance and just became an *enter* key.

By the way, on all but the very top end of typewriters, there was only one font—Courier. Center alignment? You had to plan out your words, count characters, divide by two, and move over that amount of spaces from the center of the page. Italics? Forget about it. Even early dot matrix printers had trouble with that. Ugh.

The first word processor I used was a dedicated machine—back in 1985 computers were too weak to run word processors as add-on software. Typewriters are now museum pieces, antiquated not so much for mechanical reasons but more so for the versatility and ease of word-processing software.

In today's world we type first and edit and revise later. In the days of typewriters, typing was the last thing to do because change meant retyping, and that was an unwelcome proposition. Gustave Flaubert, author of the classic *Madame Bovary*, kept notebooks full of his writing, with endless notes, cross-outs, and edits written in every available space.

Well, there's a little history lesson. It's not meant to be sentimental, but I think it helps remind us of the effort and care that should be put into the written word. In today's world of texts and tweets, of acronym jargon and auto-completion software, it's easy to forget the artistic value of the written word. When society forgets the value of a thing, society tends to lose that thing. Even so, in the age of digital timers and atomic clocks, grandfather clocks remain because of their artistic, antique charm. I'm happy to say that I own a pocket watch.

Let's hope the same will hold true for the written word and literature as a whole.

Tick-tock of the clock, click-clack of the keys, our language is more than the chatter of bees.

Reference Checklists

I N SEVERAL SECTIONS WITHIN THIS primer, there were lists of steps to outline good work practices. To make life a little easier, they are reproduced on the following pages for quick reference.

- Initial Grammar & Spelling
- Format and Submission
- Cover Letters
- Short Story Submission Formatting Standards
- Short Story Submission Checklist
- Book Query Checklist
- Press Releases
- Basic Marketing Materials
- Steps for a Simple Marketing Plan

Initial Grammar & Spelling

1. At the least use the Spell/Grammar check within your word processor—the red and green lines in your document are not Christmas decorations; they are issues that need to be addressed. At the same time, remember that a word processor uses conventional grammar rules and may not properly interpret creative or expressive forms of literal language.

2. Remember your usage of punctuation.

3. That said, remember the comma is to list items, separate ideas, link action, or lead into/out of dialog. (He said, "Go to the store." / "I will," I said.)

4. The period is a wonderful thing, but don't abuse ellipses, those three periods that indicate a trailing, incomplete thought or sentence, so ... a few of these can be used for dramatic purpose; otherwise, they say to an editor that the author didn't know how to end the narrative passage.

5. Understand the semi-colon; the semi-colon is used to link related but independent ideas or statements, as was just done.

6. Consider that, in most cases in which you might use a semi-colon, you can probably create two independent sentences that have better narrative flow. Semi-colons are more acceptable in nonfiction than fiction.

7. If you are writing fiction, it's unlikely to find any valid use or place for a colon.

8. Make sure of proper use between *to, too,* and *two*:

    to indicates a transfer or movement; go *to* the store and give money *to* the clerk.

    too indicates something in addition—think *also*; I bought some ice cream and a shovel, *too*.

    too can also indicate an extended measure; I put *too* much ice cream on my shovel.

    two ... well, it is just a number ...

9. Make sure of the proper use of *your* and *you're*:
    your as in the possessive form of *you*; that's *your* shovel.
    you're as in the contraction of *you are*; if you swing that shovel
    you're in trouble.
10. And don't forget the difference between *there*, *their*, and *they're*:
    there as in a physical or abstract location; I'm going over *there* with
    my shovel.
    their as in the possessive of individuals; that's *their* playing field
    I'm digging up.
    they're as in the contraction of *they are*; *they're* after me now that I
    dug up the field.
11. While you're at it, don't forget the difference between *its* and *it's*:
    its is the possessive form of *it*; while digging up the field I was
    drenched by *its* sprinklers.
    it's is the contraction of *it is*; those sprinklers throw so much water
    you'd think *it's* raining.
12. Why is it so important to remember the differences between these
    words? One simple answer: most spell-check tools in word processors
    fail to detect improper usage between these words.
13. Once you've gone over all of that, you might as well go back and do
    another proofread … just to be sure.

Format and Submission

1. If submitting on paper, use standard 8.5 x 11 inch white paper, printed on one side, with margins of 1 inch all around.
2. Be mindful of paragraph structure. Shifts between characters, events, and character dialog will require paragraph breaks.
3. Separate sections of narrative with a blank space, three asterisks centered, and then another blank space.
4. If you haven't already, at the minimum please do run a Spell/Grammar check!
5. No matter to whom your submission is heading, be sure to double check the submission guidelines, and make sure you adhere to the instructions.
6. It may sound silly, but be sure your contact information is on the first page of your submission and/or cover letter.
7. Even with electronic submissions, be sure you include full contact information. This includes name, pseudonym, if used, email, mailing address, and phone number.
8. By the way, this is your very last chance to find those little gaffs by using a Spell/Grammar check.

Cover Letters

1. Be sure to address the letter to the specific person—editor or agent—for your submission if one is noted in the submission instructions for the particular target—publication, publisher, or agency.

2. First paragraph should be straight to the point: the title of the story or book, the word count, and the genre.

2a. Unless instructed to do so, *do not* summarize a short story.

2b. For books, break into a new paragraph with a concise, appealing summation of the book. A good guide is to consider how the book would be encapsulated on a back cover blurb.

3. Second paragraph can contain publication credits and awards. It isn't necessary to list every achievement. If your credentials are lengthy, mention those that are most notable and/or most relevant to the publication you are targeting. For example, if it's a mystery magazine and you've published a mystery story, most certainly mention this foremost among your credentials.

4. Third paragraph can contain a short bio, two or three sentences at the most.

5. In closing you must note whether the material is a simultaneous submission or not. Some opinions state that editors, agents, and publishers with these respective policies will assume that you, as the submitting author, understand the difference. However, there are others who will reject, unread, submissions without clear statement of their non-simultaneous status. Either way it seems a simple courtesy to include this notation and a simple way to show the recipient that you did in fact read the submission guidelines.

6. Thoroughly spell and grammar check the cover letter.

7. Once the cover letter is the best it can be, keep two versions: one with an author bio and one without, as this is the most common variance in editorial instructions for cover letters. With these two files complete, they can be sent in print or copied and pasted into emails and submission managers. As you earn your publication credentials, be sure to update the letter, even with pending publication dates. It's in your favor to represent yourself as an active participant in the market.

Short Story Submission Formatting Standards

Universal Formatting

1. Always double-space.
2. Do not send handwritten work.
3. Print on one side of the page.
4. Left margin; do not justify margins.
5. Use 12 pt., Times New Roman font.
6. For new paragraphs, set a standard indentation of five spaces either with a tab or a paragraph format function.
7. Contact information on first page.
8. Header information with your name, story title, and page number.
9. If submitting by Internet, be sure to submit in the requested file type: *.doc, *.rtf, or email paste.
10. If submitting by postal mail, don't forget to include a good old SASE for editorial reply.

Standard Formatting

In addition to, or in place of, the above:

1. Use Courier, the font that looks like old style typewriter print.
2. Contact information at top left of first page, word count at top right.
3. Approximately half way down first page, story title, next line put "by," next line your name, all centered.
4. Page header, top right, with your last name/story title/page number.
5. Denote scene breaks with a single centered asterisk.
6. Do not use italics. Denote text that is to be italicized by underlining the text, excepting editor permission.
7. At story end, leave a few blank lines, and then type THE END, centered.

Online Formatting,

1. Within paragraphs, single-space. NO hard returns.
2. Use a hard return between paragraphs. In HTML this will convert to a blank line between paragraphs.

3. Denote scene breaks with three centered asterisks.
4. Do not use a double space after a period. Follow with only a single space.
5. In some cases it will be requested that paragraph indents be omitted.

Short Story Submission Checklist

1. In the most objective view, is the story the best it can be?
2. Have you run a final spell and grammar check to catch any small errors, particularly if the story just underwent an edit or revision?
3. Did you generate a word count from your word processor and identify your story's genre?
4. Determine your target market(s) and delineate between simultaneous and non-simultaneous.
5. Is the market open to submissions at this time?
6. Double check story manuscript for formatting as required by submission instructions.
7. Double check cover letter, making sure to use correct publication/editor addressee.
8. Note response time, type of submission—postal, electronic, simultaneous, etc.—in your records.

Book Query Checklist

Part A - Query letter

This restates the generalized information on cover letters, focused toward a book query package.

1. Be sure to address the letter to the specific person—editor or agent—for your submission.
2. First paragraph should be straight to the point: the title of the story or book, the word count, genre, and target audience.
3. Break into a new paragraph with a concise, appealing summation of the book. A good guide is to consider how the book would be encapsulated on a back cover blurb.
4. Third paragraph can contain a short bio, two or three sentences at the most.
5. Fourth paragraph can contain publication credits and awards. It isn't necessary to list every achievement. If your credentials are lengthy, mention those that are most notable and/or most relevant to the publication you are targeting. As with your bio, keep it short.
6. In closing you must note whether the query is a simultaneous submission or not. Some opinions state that editors, agents, and publishers with these respective policies will assume that you, as the submitting author, understand this difference. However, there are others who will reject, unread, submissions without a clear statement of their non-simultaneous status. Either way it seems a simple courtesy to include this notation and it's a simple way to show the recipient that you did in fact read the submission guidelines.
7. Thoroughly spell and grammar check the cover letter.
8. Once the letter is the best it can be, keep two versions: one with an author bio and one without, as this is the most common variance in editorial instructions for cover letters. Update the letter with new, relevant publication credentials. It's in your favor to represent yourself as an active participant in the marketplace.

Part B - Synopsis

1. Contact information, upper left of first page, with each piece of information on its own line.
2. Title, skip a line, the word SYNOPSIS, all capitals, centered beneath contact information.
3. In the header, denote the book title, the word *Synopsis*, and a page number.
4. A synopsis is always written in third person, present tense, regardless of the narrative perspective and verb tense of the book.
5. Body paragraphs. For a short—one page—synopsis, it's acceptable to single space lines within a paragraph. For a longer synopsis, stick with conventional double space.
6. The synopsis is not a strict blow-by-blow rendition of the plot; the short synopsis describes general plot and theme directions, while a full synopsis has the space to follow closer to individual plot segments.
7. Major characters, entities, and places should be written in all capitals the first time they are mentioned.

Part C - Excerpt

As per query target instructions, include first pages, first chapter, or first three chapters.

Press Releases

1. Press releases are typically no more than 300-500 words.
2. Try to keep the release limited to one page in length.
3. The release should be written in the present tense. Remember that it's breaking news, and it's ad copy.
4. National news wire services will not accept releases with heavy images or fancy graphics. In fact, no matter the distribution, aside from a simple letterhead graphic, there shouldn't be any pictures or graphics in the release.
5. If you're going to invest in a press release, consider having one written by someone experienced in ad writing. Just as writing a synopsis or pitch is very different from writing a book, so too ad copy is its own special brand of expression. Remember that you will own the release after distribution. Don't forget to include a release as part of a book press kit, book pitches, or any other promotional endeavor.

Basic Marketing Materials

1. Prepare a book fact sheet
   - This is a single, one-sided page to represent your book.
   - Include a brief synopsis, a list of relevant awards, review quotes.
   - List technical book information such as page count, print format, ISBN, publication date and publisher name.
   - Include book cover image, and, if space allows, a brief author bio.
2. Prepare a book excerpt
3. Assemble a press kit
   - The first page is a cover sheet resembling the book fact sheet, winnowed to an even tighter format to allow for a listing of the press kit contents.
   - Next page(s) for notable press release(s), followed by tear sheets of favorable market reviews.
   - The press kit does *not* include a book excerpt.
4. Design bookmarks
   - Consider one or two sided, gloss or matte finish, cardstock weight.
   - Bookmark front includes book title, book cover image, author name, ISBN, notable retail channel(s) and formats—print, Kindle, etc.—a very short synopsis, awards, perhaps a review quote or two, author website, and, if preferred, author email.
   - If two sided, the back can be used to support past publications; as space provides include cover images, synopsis, reviews and awards.
5. Craft a branding statement for your author platform.
6. Craft a product statement for your book.

Steps for a Simple Marketing Plan

1. *Create pre-buzz on social media.* Utilize your social networking accounts to start spreading word about a book's upcoming publication. Some virtual book tours offer *cover reveal* buzz packages that will tour a book's cover image with a short ad line to help build momentum.

2. *Collect market reviews.* As soon as possible, either through advanced review copies or immediately upon publication, send the book out to at least two or three professional review services. Strongly consider utilizing expedited review packages so that you can have reviews in hand for subsequent marketing steps.

3. *Assemble marketing material.* With a few reviews and perhaps a press release, it's time to put together your basic marketing tools: the book fact sheet, the book press kit, a book excerpt, bookmarks, and consider a trailer video.

4. *Submit to contests.* If finances allow, consider a few reputable award contests. Remember that contests have rolling publication date entry requirements, so if you wait too long, the book will no longer be eligible for entry. Also, early entry often means discounted entry costs.

5. *Consider a press release.* A press release of any kind can never hurt. If there is something particularly notable about the book, either from a review, an award, or a particular audience interest, sending out a release can further build momentum.

6. *Arrange a virtual book tour (VBT).* With a few reviews and marketing material in hand, consider hiring a VBT service to expose the book to bloggers. This will garner more reviews and help introduce the book to a wider reading world.

7. *Explore book launches and/or book signings.* Tap local libraries and bookstores for a night with the local community. These events may be more accessible—and more successful—when done in conjunction with a local authors group.

About the Author

A FTER MORE THAN TWENTY YEARS of hospital night shifts, Roland Allnach has witnessed life from a slightly different angle. He's been working to develop his writing career, drawing creatively from literary classics, history, and mythology.

His short stories, one of which was nominated for the Pushcart Prize, have appeared in many publications. His first anthology, *Remnant*, blending science fiction and speculative fiction, saw publication in 2010. In 2012 he followed with *Oddities & Entities*, a collection spanning the supernatural, paranormal, horror and speculative genres. His third book, *Prism*, published in 2014, follows a winding road through diverse genres and narrative forms as it explores the human experience.

Roland's books have received unanimous critical praise and have been honored with more than a dozen national book awards, including honors from National Indie Excellence, Foreword Reviews, Readers' Favorite, Feathered Quill Reviews and Pacific Book Review.

When not immersed in his imagination, Roland can be found at his website, rolandallnach.com, along with a wealth of information about his stories and experiences as an author. Writing aside, his joy in life is the time he spends with his family.

www.ingramcontent.com/pod-product-compliance
Lightning Source LLC
Chambersburg PA
CBHW072134270326
41931CB00010B/1755